the Bible story

Prince of
Princes

(From His Early Ministry to His Last Parables)

VOLUME EIGHT

the Bible Story

Prince of Princes ❖ Volume Eight

Arthur S. Maxwell
Author of Uncle Arthur's *Bedtime Stories*

When Arthur S. Maxwell wrote *The Bible Story*, he used the King James Version of the Bible, closely following its narrative. This edition continues that tradition and draws from other translations using language that today's children readily understand.

NEWLY REVISED AND ILLUSTRATED

More than 400 stories in 10 Volumes Covering the Entire Bible From Genesis to Revelation

REVIEW AND HERALD® PUBLISHING ASSOCIATION
HAGERSTOWN, MD 21740

Illustrations not individually
credited are by Corinne Boyd
Dillon, Russell Harlan,
William Heaslip, William
Hutchinson, Manning de V.
Lee, Lester Quade, Paul
Remmey, and Herbert Rudeen.

Unless otherwise noted, all
Bible verses are from the *Holy
Bible, New International Version*.
Copyright © 1973, 1978, 1983,
International Bible Society.
Used by permission of
Zondervan Bible Publishers.
Bible texts credited to TEV are
from the *Good News Bible—*
Old Testament: Copyright ©
American Bible Society 1976;
New Testament: Copyright ©
American Bible Society 1966,
1971, 1976. Bible texts credited
to RSV are from the Revised
Standard Version of the Bible,
copyright © 1946, 1952, 1971,
by the Division of Christian
Education of the National
Council of the Churches of
Christ in the U.S.A. Used by
permission.

This book was
Revised by Cheryl Holloway
Edited by Eugene Lincoln
Cover art by Harry Anderson

PRINTED IN U.S.A.

R&H Cataloging Service
Maxwell, Arthur Stanley,
1896-1970
      The Bible story.
      1. Bible stories.   I. Title.
II. Holloway, Cheryl Woolsey,
1956-

            220.9505

ISBN 0-8280-0802-7

**The pure, trusting
innocence of children
found kinship with the
gentleness and tenderness
of Jesus. Putting His hands
upon them in blessing He
said, "Of such is the
kingdom of heaven."**

PAINTING BY LARS JUSTINEN

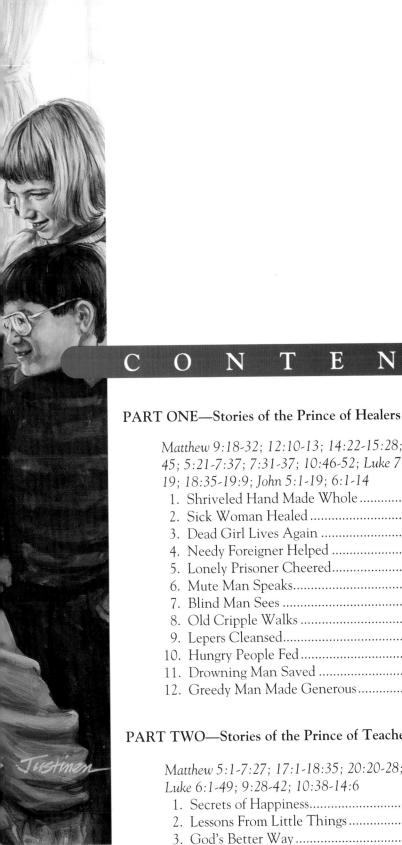

C O N T E N T S

PART ONE—Stories of the Prince of Healers

Matthew 9:18-32; 12:10-13; 14:22-15:28; 20:30-34; Mark 1:40-45; 5:21-7:37; 7:31-37; 10:46-52; Luke 7:18-35; 9:12-17; 17:11-19; 18:35-19:9; John 5:1-19; 6:1-14

PART TWO—Stories of the Prince of Teachers

Matthew 5:1-7:27; 17:1-18:35; 20:20-28; Mark 7:1-23; 10:32-40; Luke 6:1-49; 9:28-42; 10:38-14:6

PART THREE—Stories of the Prince of Storytellers

Matthew 13:1-50; 18:23-25; 21:28-22:14; Mark 12:1-44;
Luke 8:4-15; 10:25-37; 14:16-15:32; 18:9-14; 20:9-19

PART FOUR—Stories of the Prince of Prophets

Matthew 24:1-25:46; Mark 13:1-37; Luke 17:21-37; 19:12-27;
21:1-36; John 13:36-14:3

PART ONE

Stories of

the Prince of Healers

(Matthew 9:18-32; 12:10-13; 14:22-15:28; 20:30-34;
Mark 1:40-45; 5:21-7:37; 7:31-37; 10:46-52;
Luke 7:18-35; 9:12-17; 17:11-19; 18:35-19:9; John 5:1-19; 6:1-14)

Shriveled Hand Made Whole

(Luke 6:6-11)

THINGS had gone hard for the poor old man ever since he first felt the pain in his hand. He could remember the day it began. Then, as weeks and months had passed, it had become worse and worse until his finger joints were all stiff and he couldn't bend his wrist. Later his hand had gradually shriveled up until he couldn't use it at all.

That meant he couldn't work. So he had lost his job and his income, and he had even had to beg for food.

He had asked the doctors to help him, but they didn't know how to treat a shriveled hand. They had just told him he would have to put up with it for the rest of his life. It was all very sad and discouraging.

Then one Sabbath he went into the synagogue in Capernaum. As he took his seat he hid his poor hand under his robe where no one could see it. He didn't like people staring at it out of curiosity. Then he prayed the prayer he had prayed so many times before, "Dear God, help me!"

9

← PAINTING BY RUSSELL HARLAN

Jesus was the prince of healers. He entered the homes of both poor and rich, and everywhere He went He left gladness and rejoicing as a result of His wonderful healing touch.

Suddenly he became aware that for some reason or other, he had become the center of interest in the synagogue. Everybody was staring at him. He was frightened, wondering what he could have done. Surely all these people were not just looking to see his shriveled hand!

No, it couldn't be that, for he noticed that their heads kept turning from him to another Man, then back to him. The other Man was the one they called the Carpenter of Nazareth. Now the Carpenter Himself was looking at him, and he felt the warmth of friendship and sympathy in His eyes.

"Get up and stand in front of everyone," said the Carpenter in a kindly voice.

"What, me?"

"Yes, you."

Wondering what it could all mean, the poor old man, still keeping his shriveled hand covered, did as he was told. Now everybody *was* looking at him.

"Stretch out your hand," said the gentle Carpenter.

"My poor hand?"

"Yes, your poor hand."

Slowly he pulled it out from beneath his robe. Suddenly his eyes opened wide in astonishment. Then they filled with tears. For his hand wasn't shriveled anymore. It was just like his other hand! He could move his fingers! He could bend his wrist! He could touch his face! It was too good to be true, but it *was* true.

"Thank You, thank You, Master!" I can hear him saying.

But the other voices were not thankful. "He shouldn't have done it!" grumbled one.

10

"The idea of doing such a thing on the holy Sabbath!" said another.

"It's shocking," shouted a third. "The man's a lawbreaker and should be arrested."

"Which is lawful on the Sabbath: to do good or to do evil?" Jesus asked them. "To save life or to destroy it?"

No one answered Him.

As for the old man, he didn't understand what they were all arguing about. He just kept looking at his hand and moving it back and forth. He couldn't get over it. It was the best thing that had ever happened to him on the Sabbath. In the synagogue, too.

His hand had been healed! Now he could work again! Thank God! O wonderful, wonderful Jesus!

Sick Woman Healed

(Matthew 9:18-22; Mark 5:21-34)

ONE DAY as Jesus was teaching on the beach by the Sea of Galilee, He saw a man pushing his way through the crowd. The man seemed to be in a great hurry and very upset about something.

"Pardon me, please let me pass," he was saying. "I must get through to Jesus at once. Make way! *Please* make way! It's very urgent."

It was Jairus, a ruler of the synagogue, and he was troubled about his little girl. Falling to his knees before Jesus, he told Him what was the matter and earnestly begged for help. "My little daughter is dying," he cried. "Please come and put your hands on her so that she will be healed and live."

Jesus' heart was touched. He knew what it must have meant for a ruler of the synagogue to kneel and ask Him for help. How much this man loved his little girl!

"I'll go with you," said Jesus, and Jairus was delighted. But as the two started on their way, the crowd surged around them. It was hard to make any progress. So many people wanted to get close to Jesus, to look at Him, to touch Him.

They had not gone very far when suddenly Jesus stood still. "Who touched my clothes?" He asked.

It was a strange question, with so many hundreds of people pushing and shoving about Him. The disciples were surprised. "How can You ask who touched You when there are so many people around You?" they asked.

But Jesus knew somebody had touched Him. Somebody in great need. Somebody whose faith had already drawn healing power from Him. He looked around. Who of all these many, many people could it be?

Then He saw her. There was no mistaking who she was. Tears of joy and thankfulness were running down her cheeks.

Jesus understood. He smiled at her while she "fell at his feet and, trembling with fear, told him the whole truth."

She had been sick for 12 years, she said. All this long time she had gone from one doctor to another without getting any help. She had spent all her money on doctors' bills, and still her bleeding continued.

Then she had said to herself, "If I just touch his clothes, I will be healed." So she had touched Him. It was only a light

touch, on the edge of His garment. She hadn't meant to trouble Him, for she knew He was so busy looking after all the other needy people.

But then, just as soon as she had touched Him, she had felt better. Just like that. Her sickness had healed. The bleeding had stopped. She knew it for sure. And she was so thankful. So very, very thankful.

Jesus was thankful too, that somebody had trusted Him so much. "Daughter," He said to her, "your faith has healed you. Go in peace and be freed from your suffering."

The woman disappeared in the crowd, but not from history. Somebody saw and heard what happened and wrote it down, so you and I today may know that we may reach out and touch Him by faith in every time of need.

MARCUS MASHBURN

Dead Girl Lives Again

(Matthew 9:23-26; Mark 5:35-43)

WHILE all this was going on, Jairus was standing by, impatient to get back to his dying daughter. Perhaps he tugged at Jesus' sleeve, urging Him to hurry. "Please!" he may have said, "do come soon! She may die any minute."

And then she was dead.

A messenger pressed through the crowd bringing Jairus the sad news. "Your daughter is dead," he said. "Why bother the teacher any more?"

People around said, "Oh!" and began to say how sorry they were. Poor Jairus just stood there, too sad to speak. Tears rolled down his cheeks. He had loved his little girl so much!

Jesus looked at him in great pity. "Don't worry," he said, "just believe." Then He began to walk toward Jairus' house again.

What good could He do there now, Jairus thought. If only that woman hadn't stopped Him! Then He might have been in time. And what did Jesus mean by saying, "Don't worry; just believe"? The child was dead. What could anybody do but bury the poor little girl?

The crowd tried to follow Jesus, but He asked them kindly but firmly to go away. It wouldn't be proper for so many to visit a home so full of sadness. Peter, James, and John could go with Him, but no one else. He was quite strict about it, and the people obeyed Him.

As the little group came close to Jairus' house, they saw a strange sight. Many of the neighbors were trying to push their way through the front door, but they couldn't get in. The place was crowded with people. Some were friends of the family; some were just sightseers.

From inside came sounds of weeping and wailing. It was the custom in those days to employ mourners, who made sorrowful noises at funerals, and these people were "crying and wailing loudly," the Bible says.

Jesus went into the house, and Jairus and the three disciples followed. "Why all this commotion and wailing?" asked Jesus. "The child is not dead but asleep."

The mourners stopped their make-believe crying and started to laugh. "She's dead all right," one of them said. "Go and see for yourself."

"Please leave," said Jesus. And He said it so sternly that they did what He said. In a little while all of them had shuffled out the door, and the house was quiet again. Then Jesus led the sorrowing father and mother, with Peter, James, and John, into the room where the little girl was lying so white and still on her bed.

As Mother and Father sobbed in their grief, Jesus looked down at the child in great tenderness. Then He smiled at her and said, "Little girl, I say to you, get up!"

It was just as though He had said, "It's time to get up,

darling," and she woke up, right then and there. She jumped out of bed just as if she had never been sick. And I wouldn't be surprised if the first thing she said was, "Mommy, why are you crying?"

But the tears were all over now. Mother hugged her close. She didn't know whether to laugh or cry, she was so happy. So was Father. So were Peter, James, and John. And so was Jesus. He loved to make people happy. He would have liked to make every home in all the world as happy as this one was right now.

And I like to think that before He said goodbye, the little girl came up to Him and said, very sweetly and simply, out of her heart, "Thank You, kind Teacher. I love You."

Needy Foreigner Helped

(Matthew 15:21-28; Mark 7:24-30)

AFTER teaching and healing for several months in Galilee, Jesus traveled to the Mediterranean coast, then northward into Tyre and Sidon.

Here He was on foreign soil, outside the boundaries of Israel. It was just as foreign as Mexico is to the United States, or as France is to England, or as China is to Korea. The disciples must have wondered why He had come here. His message was only for the Jews, they thought. Surely He would never heal any of these Gentiles, these foreigners.

They were in for a surprise!

One day a woman followed the little group that had come with Jesus on this trip. Somehow, even this far north, she must have heard about Him and His power to heal, for she cried to Him, "Lord, Son of David, have mercy on me! My daughter is suffering terribly from demon-possession."

At first Jesus paid no attention. Perhaps this was because He wanted to see what would happen next and what His disciples would say.

But the woman continued to call to Him. "Have mercy on me! Lord, Son of David, have mercy on me! Have mercy! Have mercy!"

The disciples became annoyed. "Send her away," they urged Him, "for she keeps crying out after us."

They saw she was a foreigner. How could such a person expect any help from their Messiah? She should be sent about her business.

Then Jesus stopped walking, and the woman came close to Him. Falling at His feet she cried, "Lord, help me!"

Such a cry, no matter who gives it, whether Jew or Gentile, American or Englishman, Frenchman or German, Australian or African, always finds a response in the heart of Jesus. But this time there was a lesson for the disciples to learn first. So, speaking as they might have done, He said, "It is not right to take the children's bread and toss it to their dogs."

The woman answered, humbly and earnestly, " 'Yes, Lord,' she said, 'but even the dogs eat the crumbs that fall from their masters' table.' "

It was a wonderful answer from someone who was not an Israelite. It showed that she believed Jesus could help anyone, anywhere.

"Woman," Jesus said to her, "you have great faith! Your request is granted."

NEEDY FOREIGNER HELPED

That very moment her daughter was healed.

The disciples were astonished. Their beloved Master had answered the prayer of a foreigner! Clearly there was nothing narrow or prejudiced about Him. Could it be that He had come to bless not only "the lost sheep of Israel" but all the lost sheep of all the nations in all the wide, wide world? It was only an idea, a beautiful idea, but it began to grow and grow in their minds as the days and the years passed by.

Lonely Prisoner Cheered

(Luke 7:18-35)

WHILE Jesus was busy helping all the needy people and teaching them about His kingdom of love, He never forgot His poor cousin John, whom Herod had put in prison. His heart of love went out in pity to this mighty preacher of righteousness who was now locked up where he could never preach again.

One day two men brought Jesus a message from John, and it showed how discouraged the poor prisoner had become. "Are you the one who was to come," he asked, "or should we expect someone else?"

How different this was from what he had said about Jesus a little while before: "Look ,the Lamb of God, who takes away the sin of the world!"

It was clear that he had begun to doubt whether Jesus was really the Messiah after all. Perhaps he was wondering why He had not come long ago to set him free. But Jesus did not rebuke him. He understood how John must be feeling and how hard it is to be brave and hopeful in a dungeon.

LONELY PRISONER CHEERED

So, for John's special benefit, and to cheer his fainting heart, Jesus revealed His power as He had never done before. Quickly, "at that very time," He went from one to another of the sick people around Him, healing them of their sicknesses. He cast out evil spirits, gave sight to the blind, and gave hearing to the deaf. He even raised the dead.

Never were so many people blessed in such a short time. It was a mighty revelation of the power of God.

The two men who had come from John stood gazing open-mouthed at all these miracles. When the last sick person near Him had been healed, Jesus turned to them and told them to go and tell John all that they had seen and heard. "The blind receive sight, the lame walk, those who have leprosy are cured, the deaf hear, the dead are raised, and the good news is preached to the poor. Blessed is the man who does not fall away on account of me."

It was as if Jesus had said to John, "Cheer up! Our cause is

not lost. You may be beheaded; I may be crucified; but love will win in the end."

After John's messengers had left, their hearts full of new courage, Jesus went on to talk about His cousin to the people who remained. "What did you go out into the desert to see?" He asked them. "A reed swayed by the wind?"

John was no wind-blown reed. He was a rock of strength.

"Well, did you go out to see a man in fine clothes, living like men in the courts of kings?"

John was certainly no courtier. He was a fearless preacher of God's Word.

"Well, did you go out to see a prophet?"

Yes. That is what he was. "And much more than a prophet." And why? Because he fulfilled prophecy. He was the one Malachi had spoken about when he said, "See, I will send my messenger, who will prepare the way before me." * John prepared the way for Jesus. He was the forerunner of the Messiah.

The people who listened were happy that Jesus spoke so well of John and his work, for most of them had been baptized by him and still admired and respected him. Some of them, no doubt, carried Jesus' words to John to bring new courage to the lonely prisoner.

How glad he must have been to learn that he was not mistaken about Jesus, and that He really was "the Lamb of God" after all!

* Malachi 3:1.

Mute Man Speaks

(Mark 7:31-37)

WHEN Jesus traveled through Galilee from Tyre and Sidon to Decapolis (on the east side of the Jordan River), a deaf man who "could hardly talk" was brought to Him.

Here was a new problem. Nobody in those days knew how to help anybody like this. There were no hearing aids for the deaf or special clinics for the mute. The poor people who were handicapped like this lived in total silence, with no idea how a baby's cry might sound, or the laughter of a child, or a note of music. They could never tell their children that they loved them, or talk with their friends, or say their prayers out loud.

Even in the presence of Jesus this poor man couldn't say, "Lord, help me!" And he could not hear a word that Jesus said.

But Jesus understood. Though not a word was spoken, Jesus heard the cry in the poor man's heart. Leading him away from the crowd, He found a place where they could be alone. Then He put His fingers in the man's ears, and touched his tongue. Looking heavenward, He cried, "Be opened!" and

25

immediately the man was able both to hear and speak.

What a glorious moment that must have been for him! His whole world was changed. The years of silence were over. He could hear the birds sing and the children laugh and the voices of his neighbors as they rejoiced in his healing. And the first words he ever heard were the words of Jesus telling him to be well.

How wonderful to be able to talk like other people! For a while, I imagine, he couldn't stop talking. So much that he had wanted to say had been bottled up inside him for years. Now it came pouring out in an endless stream.

And what do you suppose he said first? Wouldn't you like to know? So would I. Somehow I think it must have been, "Jesus, O Jesus, thank You! Thank You for opening my ears and loosening my tongue. For this I will love You always."

As for the people, they were "overwhelmed with amazement. 'He has done everything well,' they said."

He surely had.

PAINTING BY PAUL REMMEY, ARTIST

Blind Man Sees

(Mark 10:46-52)

BARTIMAEUS was sitting by the roadside near the city of Jericho, begging for money from passersby. How many years he had sat in this same place day after day, he couldn't remember. It was a long, long time. Travelers between Jericho and Jerusalem had come to expect to see him here. When still quite a long way from him, they could hear his sad cry, "Help the blind! Please help the blind!"

Bartimaeus may have been blind from birth. If so, then he had never seen a flower, or a tree, or a house, or his mother's face. People would have told him about these things. He would have tried to understand what sunshine must be like, but it would have been very difficult. He lived in a world of darkness, and there was no way out.

His senses of touch and hearing were very keen, and he could find his way about very well, but he could never see anything. Nothing. Oh, how he longed to be able to see! It had been his dearest wish since his childhood. As a little boy, he had hoped that maybe when he grew up he might be able to see like other people, but now that he was old, he knew there was no hope. None.

Well, not exactly. Once, some time ago, hope had come to his heart again. It was when a passerby had told him about a wonderful Teacher who had appeared in Galilee, who was healing people of the worst diseases. He had even healed lepers and given speech to the mute and hearing to the deaf. Yes, He had even given sight to the blind.

"But don't get excited about it," the stranger had said. "He's away up in Galilee and most likely will never come to Jericho."

"Oh!" thought poor Bartimaeus, "if only He would come this way, just once!"

He thought about this many times. Now and then he would ask people whether they knew anything about the great Teacher who gave sight to the blind. Some had heard of Him and some hadn't. But nobody expected Him to come to Jericho.

"And even if He did," someone said, "He probably

wouldn't see you anyway. There are always hundreds of people around Him, all wanting something."

But, thought Bartimaeus, as hope faded again, *if He ever does come, I'll be on the roadside waiting for Him.*

Then one day it happened. It had been a warm, sunny, sultry afternoon, like so many others in this part of the Jordan valley. Very few people were traveling, and very little money had been placed in his outstretched hand. It seemed as though everybody must be staying in the city for some reason or other, and he didn't know why. Now and then he could hear shouting in the distance, but he couldn't guess what it was all about.

Then the sound grew louder, and he recognized that it was a great crowd moving. It was coming nearer and nearer along the Jericho road. He guessed there must be hundreds of people in the noisy throng, and he wondered why.

"What is it?" he asked a passerby. "What's the matter?"

"Jesus of Nazareth is passing by," said the stranger.

"Not Jesus of Nazareth!" cried Bartimaeus. Then to himself, "So He has come at last! Oh, I must not miss Him now!"

As the sound of the scuffling feet and the many voices became louder and louder, he guessed the great Teacher must be coming very near. And soon He would be gone. It was now or never.

Suddenly he shouted at the top of his voice, "Jesus, Son of David, have mercy on me!" All the longing of his soul was in that cry. All that he had hoped for through all his poor, sad life.

Nothing happened. Only more and more people went hurrying by. So he cried again as loudly as he could, "Jesus! Jesus! Son of David, have mercy on me!"

He was desperate. He *must* let Jesus know he was here. But there was so much noise. So many people. "Jesus!" he cried again, louder still.

"Be quiet!" snapped somebody. "Don't shout so! The Master's bothered enough anyway."

But Bartimaeus took no notice. This was his one great chance. It might never come again. So "he shouted all the more, 'Son of David, have mercy on me!' "

Then it seemed to him as though the crowd stopped moving. A moment later, and very close by, he heard a voice full of kindness and love saying, "Bring him to Me."

Next he heard another voice saying, "Come on, Bartimaeus. Cheer up. The Master is calling you."

Bartimaeus didn't need anyone to show him the way. The voice of Jesus drew him like a magnet.

"What do you want Me to do for you?" asked Jesus.

So Jesus had heard him! Above all the noise of the crowd the cry of one poor blind man had reached His ears!

"Rabbi," cried Bartimaeus, "I want to see!"

" 'Go,' said Jesus, 'your faith has healed you.' "

And it had, for "immediately he received his sight." His eyes opened, and the very first thing he saw was the face of Jesus smiling upon him in tender sympathy.

No wonder the Bible says that he "followed Jesus along the road." I am sure he did. All the way, to the end of life's journey.

Old Cripple Walks

(John 5:1-18)

JESUS was so eager to help the poor and needy that sometimes He searched for them wherever they could be found. One Sabbath afternoon when He was on a brief visit to Jerusalem, He went down to the pool of Bethesda to see the scores of sick folks who gathered there under its five covered colonnades.

They were a sad sight. Some were lame, some were blind, some were paralyzed. All were waiting for the water in the pool to move. No one knows what caused it, but every once in a while the water would begin to stir. Many believed that the first one into the pool after the moving of the water would be healed of whatever disease he or she had.

So day in and day out, week in and week out, each sick person at the pool kept watching the water, hoping that he or she would be the next one to be healed.

As Jesus looked at all these poor sufferers His heart of love was deeply touched. He spoke to one of them and learned that he had been a cripple for 38 years. Thirty-eight years! And all

that long, long time he had been hoping he might get better! How very, very sad!

"Do you want to get well?" asked Jesus.

Did he! But he had lost hope. "Sir," the invalid said, "I have no one to help me into the pool when the water is stirred. While I am trying to get in, someone else goes down ahead of me."

But Jesus knew how to bring new hope to the hopeless. Tenderly but firmly He said to the poor cripple, "Get up! Pick up your mat and walk."

Walk! The poor man scarcely knew what the word meant. He hadn't walked for so many, many years. He was so weak, so stiff, so—but no, he wasn't. Not anymore. Something had happened inside him. He struggled to get up. There was no pain. He found he could bend his knees. He could stand! True, he was a bit shaky, but getting steadier all the time. It was wonderful!

Then he stooped to pick up his mat, just as Jesus had told him to do, and it didn't hurt to bend. He was healed! He was well! He could walk and run and jump again—after 38 years! Wonder of wonders! It was too good to be true.

He was so excited at finding himself well that he never noticed who had healed him. When he looked around to thank Him, Jesus had gone. So he walked out onto the street—right into trouble.

← PAINTING BY PAUL REMMEY

A group of people outside asked him why he was carrying his mat on the Sabbath.

Sabbath? He had quite forgotten that it was the Sabbath, he was so happy to be healed. "The man who made me well said to me, 'Pick up your mat and walk,' " he said innocently.

"Who told you that?" they asked.

"The man who made me well."

"And who was it?" they insisted.

"I don't know."

He didn't. But a little while later, when he went to the Temple to thank God for being healed, he met Jesus again. Jesus told him not to sin anymore or else something worse might happen to him.

Then he recognized Jesus as the One who had made him well. "That's the Man!" he told those who had asked him why he was carrying his mat on the Sabbath. But they had already guessed that it was Jesus.

Foolishly they were all upset because Jesus had "broken" the Sabbath, according to their many man-made rules for keeping the day holy. They should have rejoiced that one of God's suffering children had found health and happiness on His sacred day. They needed to learn that "the Sabbath was made for man, not man for the Sabbath." *

---

* Mark 2:27.

Lepers Cleansed

(Mark 1:40-42; Luke 17:11-18)

DID YOU ever stop to think that though Jesus was always mixing with sick people, He never got sick Himself? Tired, yes, but not sick. We never read of His having mumps or measles or chicken pox or anything like that.

He was like a fountain of life, pouring out health, strength, and happiness to others. "I have come that they might have life," * He said once; and that is what He was giving away every day, all day long.

That is why people flocked to Him by the hundreds and thousands. They all wanted to be well and strong, and here was Someone who knew the secret. Better than any doctor, He was able to cure the worst diseases, and quickly, too. No sickness seemed too hard for Him. Not even leprosy.

In those days nothing frightened people more than the thought of catching this dreadful disease. Those who did had to leave their homes and villages and live with other lepers wherever they could find shelter. And they gradually got worse and worse until they died.

One day a leper, seeing Jesus in the distance, forgot all the rules about staying away from other people, and came running toward Him.

"Go away! Go away!" I can hear the bystanders crying as they moved back, scared to death. "Get out of here! You're a leper! You're unclean!"

But Jesus did not move. Instead He stood there looking down in tender pity on the poor sick man, now on his knees before Him.

"If you are willing, you can make me clean," cried the leper. And the cry came out of his heart.

What do you suppose Jesus did? He touched the leper, saying, "I am willing. Be clean!" He could have merely spoken to him, but He did more. He touched him.

The people around must have been shocked. They wouldn't have touched a leper for all the money in the Roman Empire. They were afraid that one touch might make them lepers too. But Jesus was unafraid. Life poured from Him into the poor leper, making him whole. The very moment Jesus spoke, "the leprosy left him and he was cured."

Some time later, when Jesus was passing through Samaria, He came across 10 lepers who "stood at a distance," afraid to come near Him. No doubt they had heard that He had healed

other lepers, so they cried out at the top of their voices, "Jesus, Master, have pity on us!" It was their one great chance for help, and they were not going to miss it.

Jesus heard their cry and turned toward them. His heart of love was saddened by their pitiful plight. "Go show yourselves to the priests," He called to them.

It was a strange thing for Him to say, but they understood. No leper could ever come back into society unless the priests said he was cured. So what Jesus had said meant they would be cured by the time they got to the priests.

They took Jesus at His word and started off. No doubt they kept looking at each other to see whether any change was taking place. And then it happened. Suddenly all the horrible white spots on their skin disappeared. Their half-rotted flesh became clean and whole. Their ruined features were restored,

and they looked as if they had never been sick.

"I'm healed!" cried one.

"So am I!" cried another.

"And I!" "And I!" cried the rest as they all began running to the nearest place where a priest might be found.

Jesus watched them go. Then to His great joy He saw one of them turn around and come running back to Him. Falling at Jesus' feet this man, a Samaritan, cried, "Thank You, dear Master, thank You!"

Jesus was pleased. It was good to find somebody so grateful. Turning to the people standing by He said, "Were not all ten cleansed? Where are the other nine?"

Why didn't *they* come back and say "Thank you" too?

It just shows that Jesus notices things like this. Let us be sure that we thank Him for all His goodness to us.

* John 10:10.

Hungry People Fed

(John 6:1-14)

ONE MORNING Ben had gone down to the lake with his fishing pole and caught two little fish. "Look, Mother!" he cried as he rushed into the kitchen, "See what I caught!"

Mother looked and smiled. "They're not very big, are they?" she said. "What are you going to do with them?"

"They'll do for my lunch if you'll cook them for me."

"Lunch? What are you planning to do today?"

"Oh, I'm going to listen to Jesus again. He's wonderful. You should go and hear Him too. Could I have three or four of the little barley loaves, Mother?"

"All right, dear. Take five. You'll be hungry before the day's over."

"Oh, thank you, Mother," exclaimed Ben, and in a little while he was on his way.

He had no trouble finding Jesus. Everybody seemed to know where He was. On the main road, across the fields, along the mountain trails, hundreds of excited people in small and

41

large groups were going in the same direction.

The crowd got more and more dense as Ben walked on. He had never seen so many people before. He pressed through the crowd, squeezing this way and that so he could get in front and be near the great Teacher.

Soon Jesus began to talk. And He said such beautiful things in such a kind and gentle way that the people loved every word. He spoke so clearly that even those farthest away could hear what He said.

Hour after hour slipped by. Still He talked, and still the people listened. They were so interested that they forgot all about eating. Ben even forgot to eat his lunch.

At last the sun began to sink, and a chilly breeze blew up from the lake. "Don't You think it's time to send the people home?" one of the disciples said to Jesus.

"At least let's tell them to go and buy food in the villages nearby," said another. "They haven't eaten all day."

"They don't need to go," said Jesus. "You feed them."

The disciples were shocked. "*We* don't have any food," they said.

"Eight months' wages would not buy enough bread for each one to have a bite!" said Philip.

Ben heard them talking and wondered what it was all about. Maybe Jesus was hungry, and no wonder, after talking all day. Then he thought about his lunch. "If the Master's hungry," he

said to Andrew, who was standing by, "He may have my lunch."

Andrew smiled and spoke to Jesus. "Here is a boy with five small barley loaves and two small fish," he said, "but how far will they go among so many?"

"Tell everybody to sit down," said Jesus. And they did.

"Sit down! Sit down, everybody!" the disciples shouted, moving out among the crowd.

"Why, what's the matter?" the people asked.

"We're going to eat."

"Eat? Why, where's the food?"

"Never mind. You'll see."

Ben handed his lunch to Jesus, and Jesus smiled at him saying, "Thank you, Ben, thank you very much."

That sweet smile was worth everything to Ben. It more than

made up for going without his lunch. But he didn't lose his lunch after all. Soon something very wonderful began to happen.

First, Jesus blessed the bread and the two little fish. Then He began to break them into pieces and give them to His disciples. And the strange thing was, no matter how much He broke off, there was always some left.

Pretty soon all the disciples were carrying food to the people as fast as they could walk up and down that mountainside. Time after time they came back for more, and there was always more bread and more fish waiting for them as it fell from the Master's hands.

Ben looked on amazed. He couldn't understand it. And I wouldn't be surprised if, every now and then, Jesus turned and gave him some food, just for himself. Never had he had so much to eat. He had far, far more than he would have if he had eaten his lunch all by himself.

HUNGRY PEOPLE FED

The Bible says that 5,000 men were fed that afternoon, besides women and children. And everybody had all he could eat. In fact, when it was all over, Jesus said to His disciples, "Gather the pieces that are left over. Let nothing be wasted." The meal had been so generous that the people filled 12 baskets with the leftovers.

But there's something else very special about this story. It is found in John 6:6, where we are told that Jesus "already had in mind what he was going to do." This means that right from the start, when the people began to get hungry and the disciples started to worry about how much the food would cost, Jesus had everything planned. He knew about Ben. He knew about Ben's lunch. And He knew what He would do with it if Ben would give it to Him.

He had watched Ben all day. He had seen how interested he was. He knew Ben wanted to do something for Him. And so He planned the whole marvelous miracle with this little boy in mind!

Today He has His eye on *you*. Perhaps, who can tell, He is planning to do something great and wonderful with you. He knows what He would do if you would let Him, if you would place your best, your dearest treasure, in His hands.

Drowning Man Saved

(Matthew 14:22-33)

FEEDING all those people must have put a great strain on Jesus and His disciples. In fact, the disciples were so tired after carrying all that food to the 5,000 people that Jesus told them to get in a boat and sail to the other side of the lake for a rest.

Meanwhile He tried to send the people home. It was difficult, for some of them wanted to make Him a king then and there. A man who could provide free meals like this was the very person they were looking for to be the king of Israel. But Jesus did not want to be that kind of king, so He told them to leave Him alone. At last, after much coaxing, they went away. Then He climbed the mountainside again and prayed.

Later that night a storm came up. Remembering His disciples out on the lake, Jesus decided to go to them. So He went down to the shore and kept right on walking across the lake. How He did it, nobody knows, but somehow he walked on the water, because all the disciples saw Him.

And were they scared! "It's a ghost!" they cried as the

47

When Peter saw Jesus walking on the water, he stepped boldly out of the boat to meet Him, but when he got his eyes off the Saviour, and felt himself sinking, he cried, "Lord, save me!"

white form of the Master appeared, walking calmly over the waves.

"It is I. Don't be afraid," Jesus called them.

They couldn't believe their ears or their eyes. How could Jesus be out there on the water with no boat under Him?

Peter was always ready with a bright idea. "Lord, if it's you," he called, "tell me to come to you on the water."

"Come!" said Jesus.

Probably Peter didn't expect such an answer. But now he clambered over the side of the boat and started to go to his beloved Master. That took a lot of courage on such a dark night and a rough lake. But Peter was well rewarded.

This was wonderful! He was actually walking on water, just as Jesus was. He hadn't thought it possible. Why hadn't he tried it before?

But his joy and courage didn't last long. Taking his eyes off Jesus, he began to look around at the waves. What if one of them knocked him over? What if he couldn't keep his footing? He began to doubt. And that very moment he began to sink.

"Lord, save me!" he cried.

In a flash Jesus was by his side, holding him up. " 'You of little faith,' he said, 'why did you doubt?' "

As the two stepped over the side of the boat the lake suddenly became calm. So did the disciples. Remembering the miracle of yesterday, and now this, they fell on their knees before Him crying, "Truly you are the Son of God."

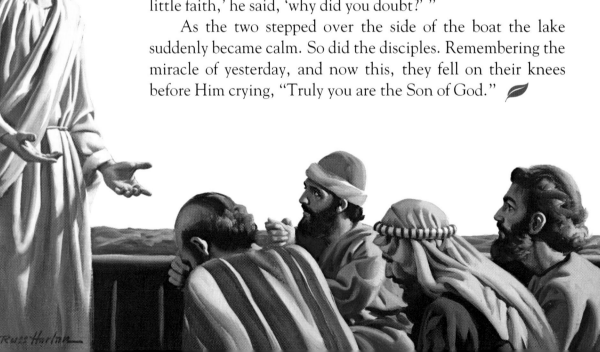

Greedy Man Made Generous

(Luke 19:1-10)

NOT ONLY did Jesus heal the sick, cleanse lepers, restore cripples, give sight to the blind, make the deaf hear, feed the hungry, save the drowning, and raise the dead, but He somehow got right inside people's minds and hearts, and led them to think and act like new men and women. He was the Prince of healers.

Passing through Jericho one day with a big crowd of people around Him, His keen eyes caught sight of a very short man running ahead of the crowd. It was Zacchaeus, the chief tax collector of the district, who was very rich.

Zacchaeus ran on until he got to a sycamore-fig tree. There, forgetting his importance, he climbed the tree like a boy and made himself comfortable in the branches.

Jesus was glad that such a man as this was interested enough to go to all this trouble just to catch a glimpse of Him as He passed by. The crowd moved slowly on, with some people shoving hard to get closer to Jesus and others

calling loudly to Him for help. At the sycamore-fig tree Jesus stopped and looked up into the face of Zacchaeus.

The tax collector was delighted. Here was the great Teacher of Galilee right underneath him, looking up at him—yes, smiling at him! Something began to happen inside him then and there. Surely, he thought, Jesus couldn't be interested in *him*. Not in a tax collector. Everybody hated tax collectors.

But Jesus *was* interested in him. Very much so. To the

surprise of Zacchaeus and everybody else around, Jesus said, "Zacchaeus, come down immediately. I must stay at your house today."

"My house?" asked Zacchaeus, his eyes opening wide in surprise and a smile wreathing his face. "My house?"

The next moment he had slid down the tree and was standing beside Jesus. "Do come! You are so welcome," he said, and proudly led Jesus to his home.

The people in the crowd couldn't understand it. They began to complain that Jesus had left them to go off with a tax collector, of all people!

But Jesus knew what He was doing. He could see all the hidden good in this little man, good that was waiting for love to bring out.

It was a fine house they went into, one of the best on the outskirts of Jericho. No doubt it had a beautiful view over the Jordan valley. Zacchaeus was so pleased that the great Teacher had been willing to come to his home that he ordered his servants to bring cool drinks and the best of food for his Guest.

I wish I knew all that Jesus said to Zacchaeus as they sat together in the living room, or maybe on the porch, that day. But I don't. All we know is that before the afternoon was over, Zacchaeus was a changed man.

"Jesus," he said, "I've made up my mind. I'm going to give

51

half of all I own to the poor. And if I've ever cheated anyone, I'm going to give back four times the amount."

Jesus was delighted. "Today salvation has come to this house," He said. Then He spoke those words that have brought so much blessing to millions of people ever since: "For the Son of man came to seek and to save what was lost."

Yes. Rich and poor. High and low. Sick and well. Old and young. The tax collector and those who are taxed. Anybody who is lost, who wants to find the way home to God and heaven, may know that Jesus is seeking him and will save him if he wants to be saved.

Wherever you are—up a tree, in a boat, on a city street, or in your bedroom at home—Jesus is looking for you. 🖋

PART TWO

Stories of

the Prince of Teachers

(Matthew 5:1-7:27; 17:1-18:35; 20:20-28;
Mark 7:1-23; 10:32-40; Luke 6:1-49; 9:28-42; 10:38-14:6)

Secrets of Happiness

(Matthew 5:3-12)

JESUS was not only the Prince of healers, He was the Prince of teachers, too. He had something on His heart that He wanted to tell people, and He told it so simply and clearly that most of them loved every word. They listened to Him as long as He would talk to them.

He had come from heaven to tell them about God. He was eager for them to know that God is a God of love. He is kind, patient, and forgiving, yet at the same time He is a holy God who wants His children be good, pure, truthful, and obedient.

He often talked about His coming kingdom and what a happy place it will be—a place where everybody will love everybody else and nobody will ever do anything wrong, unkind, or mean.

Anybody, just anybody, could belong to His kingdom, as long as he believed in Jesus and was willing to do as He said. And he didn't have to wait a long, long time to enjoy the happiness of that kingdom. He could have it now. Certain of God's love, sure of His watchcare, the believer in Jesus could

55

← PAINTING BY HERBERT RUDEEN

As the people sat around Jesus on the hillside, He told them of His coming kingdom and of the home being prepared for those redeemed through faith in His sacrifice on Calvary.

live without a single worry, his heart forever bubbling over with joy and peace.

This is what Jesus meant when, sitting on the mountainside one day, He said to the people who were gathered around Him:

"Blessed are the poor in spirit, for theirs is the kingdom of heaven.

"Blessed are those who mourn, for they will be comforted.

"Blessed are the meek, for they will inherit the earth.

"Blessed are those who hunger and thirst for righteousness, for they will be filled.

"Blessed are the merciful, for they will be shown mercy.

"Blessed are the pure in heart, for they will see God.

"Blessed are the peacemakers, for they will be called sons of God.

"Blessed are those who are persecuted because of righteousness, for theirs is the kingdom of heaven.

"Blessed are you when people insult you, persecute you and falsely say all kinds of evil against you because of me.

"Rejoice and be glad, because great is your reward in heaven, for in the same way they persecuted the prophets who were before you."

In these wonderful words Jesus told the secrets of true happiness. To be blessed, to be truly happy, depends, He said, on how we live before God.

SECRETS OF HAPPINESS

If we—you and I—keep humble and never let pride come into our hearts, the kingdom of heaven will be ours—not only in the future, but now.

If we are truly sorry for our sins, and "mourn" for them because they offend God, He will comfort us with His forgiveness.

If with all our hearts we long to be good, God will bless our lives with victory over all temptations.

If we are kind and merciful to others, we shall have the joy of seeing them merciful to us.

If we keep our hearts pure and refuse to think evil thoughts, our minds will be clear to understand God and be ready to receive the happiness He wants to give us.

If we try to be peacemakers, loving others instead of fighting them, all sorts of blessings will be ours; but, best of all, we will know for sure that we are the children of God.

If we get into trouble for doing right and are misunderstood for following God's way, we do not need to worry. Everything will come out right in the end. His kingdom is ours, now and forever.

We can be happy even when people try to do us harm. No matter how mean they become, we can "rejoice and be glad," for God knows all about it and is preparing a great reward for us in heaven. 🖋

Lessons From Little Things

(Matthew 5:13-16; 6:25-34; 7:7-11)

MOST of the people who came to listen to Jesus had never been to school. Many of them could not read or write. In the crowds that followed Him were some priests and Levites and a few well-to-do people who had been to the schools of the rabbis. But the farmers, the cattlemen, the shepherds, the vineyard workers, the stonemasons, the carpenters, and the housewives, knew very little beyond what they had been told by their parents or had heard in the synagogues from Sabbath to Sabbath.

That is why Jesus made His teaching so simple, and why "the common people heard Him gladly" (KJV).[1] He talked about salt and oil lamps, baskets and flowers, pigs and pearls, seeds and weeds, grapes and figs, sparrows and eagles, narrow gates and wide gates. It was from these simple, everyday things that He drew some of His most important lessons.

Salt was plentiful in the Jordan valley. From where they were sitting, perhaps the people could see it gleaming white in

the sunshine. They all knew it was used to make things taste better and to preserve them.

"You should be like that," Jesus told the people. "God wants you to be the salt of the earth, making life happier for others, setting them a good example, standing always for the right."

Everybody knew what Jesus was talking about when He spoke of an oil lamp. That's all the light they had in their homes, for of course there were no gas or electric lights in those days. And when Jesus asked them if they covered a lighted lamp with a bowl, I can imagine they all smiled and said, "Of course not!"

"I'm sure you don't," Jesus said. "You put it on a lamp stand so that it will light your house." Then He added, "Let your light shine before men, that they may see your good deeds and praise your Father in heaven."

They got His point. He wanted all the love and kindness He put in their hearts to shine like a light in the dark, and in this way they would be the "light of the world." But this was not to

call attention to themselves, but to God, the source of all goodness and love.

A little later on He talked about the birds that were flying around. "Look at them," He said. "They don't plant seeds, or reap harvests, or gather grain into barns. Yet your heavenly Father feeds them. Why worry about what to eat? Your Father in heaven loves you even more! Don't you think He will take care of you?"

Then He pointed to the flowers growing at His feet on the mountainside. "See how the lilies of the field grow," He said. "They do not labor or spin. Yet I tell you that not even Solomon in all his splendor was dressed like one of these." Then came this lesson: "If that is how God clothes the grass of the field, . . . will he not much more clothe you, O you of little faith?"

He was trying to take all the worry out of their lives, for people worried just as much in those days as they do now. They did not need to keep asking " 'What shall we eat?' or 'What shall we drink?' or 'What shall we wear?' " And why? Because, Jesus said, "Your heavenly Father knows that you need them."

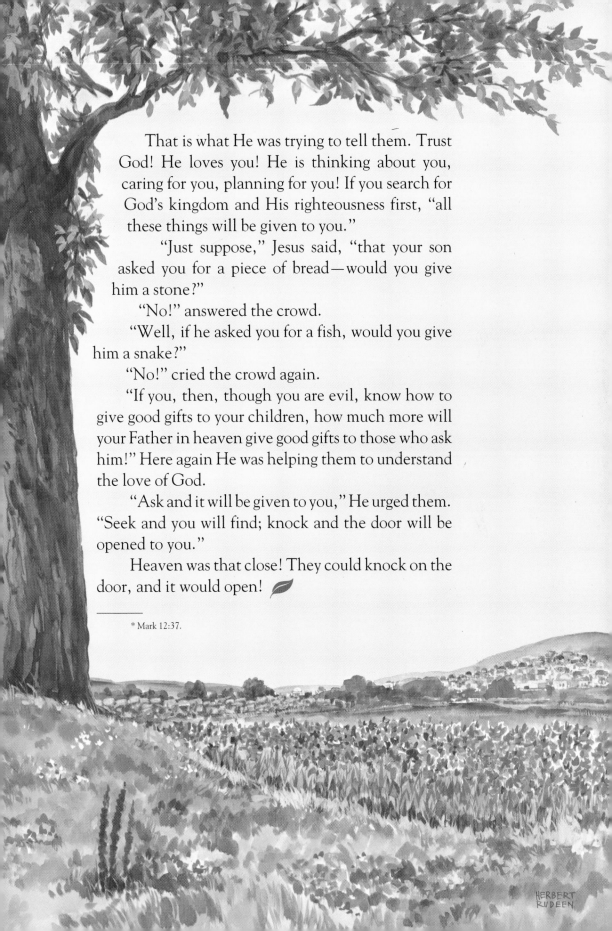

That is what He was trying to tell them. Trust God! He loves you! He is thinking about you, caring for you, planning for you! If you search for God's kingdom and His righteousness first, "all these things will be given to you."

"Just suppose," Jesus said, "that your son asked you for a piece of bread—would you give him a stone?"

"No!" answered the crowd.

"Well, if he asked you for a fish, would you give him a snake?"

"No!" cried the crowd again.

"If you, then, though you are evil, know how to give good gifts to your children, how much more will your Father in heaven give good gifts to those who ask him!" Here again He was helping them to understand the love of God.

"Ask and it will be given to you," He urged them. "Seek and you will find; knock and the door will be opened to you."

Heaven was that close! They could knock on the door, and it would open!

---

* Mark 12:37.

God's Better Way

(Matthew 5:17-45)

A

S JESUS talked to the people He seemed to be saying, "I know a better way for you to live. And if you will try to live My way—God's way—you will be so much happier."

His way, of course, was the way of love, and He tried to make it plain to those who came to listen to Him. "You have heard," He said, "that it was said to the people long ago, 'Do not murder, and anyone who murders will be subject to judgment.' But I tell you that anyone who is angry with his brother will be subject to judgment."

Here was a new idea. It was not only wrong to kill, but it was wrong even to be angry. In fact, Jesus said, just calling your brother a fool is displeasing to God. And why? Because it isn't the way of love.

Love is kind, gentle, polite, forgiving. Boys and girls with love in their hearts will never say or do mean things to other children, but will do and say things to make them happy.

Again, Jesus said, "You have heard that it was said to the

62

people long ago, 'Do not break your oath, but keep the oaths you have made to the Lord.' But I tell you, Do not swear at all: either by heaven, for it is God's throne; or by the earth, for it is his footstool; or by Jerusalem, for it is the city of the Great King."

This was another new idea. The people knew that it was wrong to swear that something was true when it really wasn't. But it had never occurred to them that God might be just as displeased with ordinary foolish swearing. But He is, said Jesus, and those who love Him with all their hearts will never take His name in vain like this.

Now Jesus brought out yet another new, very startling idea. "You have heard that it was said, 'Eye for eye, and tooth

for tooth.' But I tell you, Do not resist an evil person. If someone strikes you on the right cheek, turn to him the other also.
And if someone wants to sue you and take your tunic, let him
have your cloak as well. If someone forces you to go one mile, go
with him two miles."

This was hard to take. No doubt many in the crowd were
thinking, "If I could just get hold of so-and-so, I'd treat him as
he treated me." Now they knew they must never think such
thoughts again. God's better way was the way of forgiveness, of
turning the other cheek, of giving the tunic with the coat, and
of going the second mile.

Now Jesus went still further, saying, "You have heard that
it was said, 'Love your neighbor and hate your enemy.' But I tell
you: Love your enemies and pray for those who persecute you,
that you may be sons of your Father in heaven."

"What!" I can hear someone asking, "Do you mean to say
we are to love the Romans, the tax collectors, and everybody
else who tries to rob us and do us harm?"

"Yes," said Jesus, "everybody. Just as the sun shines on the
good and the evil and the rain falls on the righteous and the

unrighteous, so you are to love your enemy as well as your friend."

Some thought that Jesus was trying to do away with all the old laws they had heard about in the synagogue.

"Oh, no," He said. "Do not think that I have come to abolish the Law or the Prophets; I have not come to abolish them but to fulfill them."

There was nothing the matter with the law; it was the way they were trying to keep it that was wrong. The only way the law could ever be kept was in a spirit of love. If their hearts were full of love, if they loved God with all their mind and soul and strength, and if they loved their neighbors as much as they loved themselves, they would have done all the law asked of them.

It is love that matters most to God. This is His better way, the way to real, lasting happiness.

We must try to follow this better way today.

How to Pray

(Matthew 6:5-13)

MANY of the people who listened to Jesus did not know how to pray. Some of them had never prayed in all their lives.

This was the cause of their sorrows, their worries, their failures. Jesus knew that. So He tried to get them to think of God as their Friend and to talk to Him as to one who loved them and was interested in them. How could they live the good life and walk God's better way if they never asked Him for help?

Jesus Himself prayed often. Sometimes He would spend a whole night in prayer, talking with His heavenly Father and seeking help for the great work He had come to the earth to do.

Once when He looked up from praying, He found some of His disciples standing by, watching Him. They had been listening to His simple, beautiful words as He talked with His Father, and they wished they could pray like that.

"Lord, teach us to pray," they said, and Jesus was pleased. He had hoped that they would ask that question. Now He could tell them the secret of prayer and they would listen and remember.

First of all, He said, they should not pray just so other people would think they were religious and good. Long, loud prayers in public to be "seen by men" aren't prayers at all. They don't reach heaven. God doesn't hear them.

"When you pray," He said, "go into your room and shut the door." Prayer is something very private, just between you and God.

"And when you pray," He said, "do not keep on babbling like pagans." Don't feel you must keep saying the same words over and over. Just talk as you would to a friend.

Then He taught them the little prayer that has become known to millions upon millions of people all over the world as the Lord's Prayer. "Our Father in heaven, hallowed be your name, your kingdom come, your will be done on earth as it is in heaven. Give us today our daily bread. Forgive us

our debts, as we also have forgiven our debtors. And lead us not into temptation, but deliver us from the evil one."

From the first word to the last it is the perfect prayer. It turns our thoughts heavenward. It makes us think of God, His holiness, His kingdom, His power, His glory. And all it asks for ourselves is our daily bread, a forgiving spirit, and strength to overcome evil.

There is not a single selfish request. Even those that mention our needs are for the glory of God. We ask for His blessings so we can help in His plans for His kingdom of love.

We should learn this prayer and say it often. Yet it is not the only prayer we should pray. For God is our Friend, and He wants us to tell Him all that is in our hearts. He wants to hear how much we love Him, how earnestly we want to please Him, how much we need His help to do what is good and true and right, and how eagerly we want to serve Him all the days of our lives.

Treasures in Heaven

(Matthew 6:19-21)

I N THOSE long-ago days when Jesus was teaching in Galilee there were no banks like we have in every city today. If a man had something valuable he wanted to keep very safely, he put it in a hole in the ground or in a cellar under his house.

But even the best hiding places were not very safe. If they were damp, then the precious object became rusty or tarnished. If they were dry and the treasure was a beautiful garment, or a priceless picture, or a valuable piece of furniture, then moths or worms or termites could destroy it. And there was always the danger that thieves might break in and steal it, or an invading army might carry it away.

There simply wasn't any safety anywhere, and Jesus pointed out to the people how foolish it was for them to spend so much time saving money to buy things that wouldn't last or that couldn't be kept very long, or that could be so easily stolen.

"Do not store up for yourselves treasures on earth, where moth and rust destroy, and where thieves break in and steal,"

70

He said. "But store up for yourselves treasures in heaven." Treasure stored in heaven is safe forever. No moths, no rust, no thieves, can get in there.

The people must have looked at Him with a puzzled expression on their faces. What did He mean? How could anybody put treasures in heaven? Perhaps somebody called out, "You mean I can put my money in heaven and it will be safe from robbers?"

"Yes."

"But how?"

"By giving it to somebody in need."

Everybody must have smiled. This seemed so foolish. Yet it wasn't. It was very, very true. Because, you see, when we use our treasure in a spirit of love to help others, we really give it to God. And God, who never forgets a single good deed done in His name, in some way will repay our gift, and often it is much more than we could ever wish for.

"Give to others, and God will give to you," said Jesus. "Indeed, you will receive a full measure, a generous helping, poured into your hands—all that you can hold. The measure

you use for others is the one God will use for you" (TEV).

Love puts the treasure in heaven and love pays it out again.

Of course it takes faith to put money—or anything else—into this kind of bank. But it takes faith to put money in any kind of bank, doesn't it? Of course it does! Even a piggy bank!

So to make this new kind of banking work, you have to believe in God and heaven, and in love—which is the only kind of money heaven knows.

"Where your treasure is," said Jesus, "there your heart will be also." If your treasure is in your basement, or anywhere else on earth, you'll be forever worrying about it. But if you use it in love to the glory of God, you will put it in heaven; and your heart, following it there, will find the peace and happiness that heaven alone can give.

House on a Rock

(Matthew 7:24-27; Luke 6:47-49)

AS JESUS came to the end of His long sermon about the love of God, He drew another striking word picture which was so simple and clear that everybody understood it at once.

It was a story of two houses—one built on rock, the other on sand. Both looked alike; both seemed good to live in. Then a storm came up, and a flash flood filled the riverbed. One house stood, but the other fell and was swept away.

Everybody listening to Him, Jesus said, was building on one kind of foundation or the other. Those who made up their minds to follow His teaching and let the love of God fill their hearts and rule their lives were like the man who "dug down deep and laid the foundation on rock."

On the other hand, some had refused to obey His teachings and had decided to go on living the same old kind of life with all its meanness and littleness. They were "like a man who built a house on the ground without a foundation."

73

In the days ahead fierce storms would blow on all their houses. Big floods of trouble would come to them. That time of testing would expose the kind of foundation they had built on.

Nothing will ever hurt the girl or boy whose life is built on love, for love—though it cannot be seen with your eyes or felt with your fingers—is like a rock. It lasts. It is eternal, like God Himself. Those who have hearts full of love, who live for others, become so wrapped up in God's plans for the future that they just go on with God forever and ever.

On the other hand, the shallow little people who think only of themselves cannot endure trouble. They go all to pieces. They have no future, for they have no love.

What are you planning to build your house on? Sand? Or rock?

If you want it to stand forever, dig deep. The Rock is there.

Good Deeds on a Good Day

(Mark 2:23-28; Luke 13:10-17; 14:1-6)

T HE MORE Jesus talked about His kingdom of love, the more He seemed to get into trouble with the religious leaders of His day.

Because He said that loving people and being kind to them was more important than all the rules of conduct anybody ever made, they said He was a rebel. They spread the story that He was against all religion because He was against *their kind* of religion. And oh, how they watched Him to see if He would break another of their rules!

One Sabbath day Jesus walked through the grainfields with His disciples. Being hungry, they picked some heads of grain, rubbed them in their hands, and ate the kernels.

"Sabbathbreakers!" muttered some Pharisees who were looking on. To them this was as bad as harvesting a whole grainfield on the Sabbath. "Why are they doing what is unlawful on the Sabbath?" they demanded.

But Jesus was ready for them.

"Haven't you read about David?" He said, reminding them

of the time when David, fleeing from Saul, went into the tabernacle, ate the holy bread, and gave some to those who were with him.

The Pharisees remembered all right, and they didn't know what to say about it. So Jesus said to them, "The Son of Man is Lord . . . of the Sabbath."

This must have been a big shock, for it was as if He had said, "I made the Sabbath, and I am the One to say how it should be kept."

If it had been wrong for the disciples to pick those heads of grain on the Sabbath, Jesus would have said so — but it wasn't wrong. They weren't *working*, but getting necessary food in a very simple way, just as you eat your breakfast or lunch on the Sabbath today.

The same question came up over and over again. On another Sabbath, as Jesus was speaking in a synagogue, He noticed a poor woman all doubled up from some terrible disease. She had been like this for 18 years, and nobody had ever been able to help her.

Touching her gently, Jesus said, "Woman, you are free from your sickness."

At once she stood up straight, her face radiant with joy and gratitude. But the ruler of the synagogue was furious. Turning to the people around him, he said, "There are six days for work. So come and be healed on those days, not on the Sabbath."

Jesus looked around. "You hypocrites!" He said sternly. "Doesn't each of you on the Sabbath untie his ox or donkey from the stall and lead it out to give it water? Then should not this woman, a daughter of Abraham, whom Satan has kept bound for eighteen long years, be set free on the Sabbath day from what bound her?"

This made the ruler of the synagogue ashamed, for good reason. But the rest of the people "were delighted with all the wonderful things he was doing."

On yet another Sabbath, when dining in the home of one of the chief Pharisees, Jesus noticed that one of the men present had dropsy. So He asked the Pharisees and lawyers

77

who were there, "Is it lawful to heal on the Sabbath or not?"

They didn't answer. So He healed the man on the spot. Then He asked another question: "If one of you has a son or an ox that falls into a well on the Sabbath day, will you not immediately pull him out?"

Again nobody answered.

Perhaps Jesus looked all along the row of puzzled, angry faces, as if saying, "Well, how about you—and you?—and you?"

Of course they would help their animals on the Sabbath! Some of them had done it many times. Yet they thought it was a sin to heal a poor sick man! How mixed up they all were!

Of course it is right to do good on the Sabbath day. As Jesus said time and time again, "The Sabbath was made for man"— for his good, his happiness, his welfare—"not man for the Sabbath."

Glimpse of the Kingdom

(Matthew 16:28-17:13; Luke 9:27-36)

ONE DAY Jesus said a very strange thing to His disciples. "Some who are standing here will not taste death before they see the Son of Man coming in his kingdom."

You can imagine how they must have looked at each other, wondering what He meant and who the fortunate ones would be. Did He mean that before all the disciples would die, He would begin His reign as King of love in all the world? If so, how wonderful!

But Jesus didn't mean that at all. He had something else in mind. As it turned out, the fortunate ones were Peter, James, and John. Jesus took them off by themselves and led them up a high mountain, possibly Mount Hermon, which is almost always snowcapped.

Up, up, up the steep slope they followed their beloved Master until they were weary with the climb. When at last, near the summit, Jesus stopped, they were ready to lie down and sleep. In fact, they were so sleepy that they almost missed the

most wonderful sight that human eyes ever saw.

They had often seen Jesus praying before, but never like this! His face was glowing with a glorious, heavenly light. His clothes were glistening as when the sun shines on pure white snow. He looked like a king—but more than a king. Yes, He looked like God!

Then they saw something else that startled them. From nowhere, it seemed, two strangers appeared and stood by Jesus.

The disciples stared at them. Could they be angels? No. They were men all right. There was no doubt about that. But who were they? And how had they come so suddenly to this mountaintop?

The disciples had no way of knowing who these two people might be. They had never seen pictures of them. But Jesus knew them and talked with them as if they were old friends of His, which they were. One was Moses, and the other was Elijah.

But weren't these two people dead?

No. After Moses died on Mount Nebo, God raised him from the dead, as we understand from the book of Jude. As for Elijah, he never died, but was taken to heaven in a chariot of fire.

So here on this mountaintop Jesus gave His three most trusted disciples a picture of what is going to happen in that glorious day when He will return to set up His kingdom.

On that happy morning He will appear in all His glory as King of kings and Lord of lords. Then all who have died believing in Him will be raised to life—as Moses was—and those still living will be caught up in the clouds to meet Him in the air, like Elijah.

← PAINTING BY HERBERT RUDEEN

Suddenly while Peter, James, and John prayed on the mountainside with Jesus, He was enveloped with the dazzling light of heaven, and two men, Moses and Elijah, appeared at His side.

After a little while Moses and Elijah vanished. When they were gone, Peter said to Jesus, "If you wish, I will put up three shelters—one for you, one for Moses and one for Elijah."

It was a foolish thing to say. In very sacred moments like this it is always good to keep quiet and say nothing.

Jesus did not answer. And a moment later a cloud came down and covered them. From the cloud came a voice, rich, beautiful, and full of melody, and it said, "This is my Son, whom I love; with him I am well pleased. Listen to him!" Again God claimed Jesus as His Son, as He had done once before by the Jordan.

Terrified, the three disciples "fell face down to the ground." How long they stayed like this, we do not know, but eventually each one felt a familiar touch on the shoulder. "Get

LARS JUSTINEN

up," said Jesus gently. "Don't be afraid."

They looked up and "saw no one except Jesus."

Why did Jesus let Peter, James, and John have this wonderful experience?

Because He knew they would need it in the sad, trying years ahead. It would help to keep up their courage when His cause would appear to be lost and everything would seem to go wrong.

The Prince of teachers was right. The disciples never forgot that marvelous sight on the mountain. Long years afterward Peter wrote about it, saying, "We were eyewitnesses of His majesty." [1] And John, in the first chapter of his Gospel, said, "We have seen His glory, the glory of the One and Only, who came from the Father." [2]

For the rest of their lives this was one of their most precious and sacred memories.

---

[1] 2 Peter 1:16.
[2] John 1:14.

Why the Power Failed

(Matthew 17:14-20; Luke 9:37-43)

UNFORTUNATELY, when the four reached the foot of the mountain again, they didn't find any glory there. Instead they found the other disciples in a very difficult situation. They had met their first failure and didn't know what to do about it.

You see, a little while before this, Jesus had called His 12 disciples together and had given them power "to drive out all demons and to cure diseases." Then He had "sent them out to preach the kingdom of God and to heal the sick." *

At first they had been very happy about this. They were thrilled to find that they were able to perform miracles of healing just as their Master did. And when they found that even the demons obeyed them, their joy knew no bounds.

This was wonderful! Humble fishermen from Galilee commanding demons to come out of people, and the demons doing as they were told! Day after day the miracles continued, with the disciples

84

becoming bolder and bolder as they traveled about the country, bringing health and happiness to the needy.

Then came the sad day when all of a sudden the power didn't work anymore. They found themselves as helpless as the people they were trying to heal.

A man had brought his demon-possessed son for healing, and the disciples had commanded the evil spirit to leave the boy—but nothing happened. They tried again and again, and still nothing happened. The boy raved on.

The poor father was bitterly disappointed. So were the disciples. What was the matter? they wondered. What had gone wrong? Why didn't the power of God work in this case?

About this time some of the people in the crowd caught

sight of Jesus with Peter, James, and John, coming down the mountain.

"There He is!" they cried. "He'll know what to do!" And, of course, He did.

The boy's father was so anxious to get help for his boy that he ran toward Jesus. "Teacher, I beg you to look at my son, for he is my only child," he cried.

Then he told Jesus all about the boy: how the demons would throw him into the fire or into water, and there was nothing anybody could do for him. Not even the disciples. "I begged your disciples to drive it out," he said, "but they could not."

"Bring him to Me," said Jesus.

The father took the boy's hand and tried to lead him over to where Jesus was standing, but just then the boy fell on the ground in a convulsion. Jesus took one look at the pitiful sight, then commanded the demon to come out of him. The demon obeyed, and the boy "was healed from that moment."

Those who saw the miracle were "amazed at the greatness of God," but the disciples were very upset. Jesus had succeeded where they had failed, and they were ashamed. What *was* the

matter? they kept asking themselves. Had they said the wrong words, or what?

When everybody else had gone away they came to Jesus and asked Him, "Why couldn't we drive it out?"

"Because you have so little faith," said Jesus.

If they had just the tiniest bit of faith—as small as a mustard seed—He told them, they would be able to say to a whole mountain of trouble, "Go away!" and it would go. Nothing would be impossible for them.

Wouldn't it be wonderful to have faith like this and be able to do "impossible" things for God? It certainly would. And you may have it if you pray for it and want it for God's glory, not yours.

The real trouble with the disciples that day was that each of them wanted to be the greatest. I wouldn't be surprised if they had been adding up the miracles God had worked through each of them and comparing one with another to see who had done the most!

No wonder the power had stopped flowing! No wonder the devil had been able to get the better of them! No wonder their faith had shriveled up until it was so small God couldn't find enough of it to use to save this one poor demon-possessed boy!

The channels of our hearts must be clear of all pride, all selfishness, all self-importance, before the power of God can flow through them in all its fullness.

---

* Luke 9:1, 2.

Money in a Fish

(Matthew 17:24-27; 22:15-22)

EVEN though Jesus tried His best to love people and be kind to them, there were always some around Him who didn't want to be loved. They disliked Him because He was so popular, and they hated Him because He was so good.

It happens like that at school sometimes. The bad boys bully those who behave themselves, and the lazy ones are mean to the ones who study hard and get good grades.

Jesus' enemies were always trying to trick Him into saying or doing something that would get Him into trouble. One day a group came to Him and, trying to appear very innocent, asked, "Is it right to pay taxes to Caesar?"

Jesus saw the trap at once. If He said No, the Romans would arrest Him for treason. If He said Yes, the people who hated the Romans would have a case against Him.

So He didn't say Yes or No. He merely asked for a coin and pointed to the face on it. "Whose portrait and inscription is this?" He asked.

"Caesar's," they said, wondering at His question.

"Give to Caesar what is Caesar's," He replied, "and to God what is God's."

It was up to them to decide which things belong to Caesar and which belong to God. This was too hard for them, "so they left him and went away."

Another time the tax collectors in Capernaum asked Peter whether his Master paid the Temple tax.

"Yes," said Peter, hurrying home to tell Jesus what they had said to him.

Jesus did not need to pay this particular tax since He was a teacher. If He paid it, his authority as a teacher could be questioned. If He did not, He would appear disloyal to the Temple. His enemies were sure they had Him cornered.

But Jesus could not be tricked this way. He told Peter to do a very unusual thing. "So that we may not offend them," He said, "go to the lake and throw out your line." Jesus promised that the first fish he would catch would have a piece of money in its mouth.

Off Peter went with his line and hook. Though he had

fished all his life, this was the strangest fishing trip he had ever been on. Arriving at the beach, he baited the hook and threw it as far from the shore as he could. Then he waited. Soon he felt a sharp tug. His line tightened. He pulled on it sharply to set the hook, then carefully hauled in his catch. Soon he could see a fish jumping and splashing about in the water.

"This must be it!" he said to himself. "The Master said it would be the first one." Grabbing the fish in both hands, he forced its mouth open. Inside was a four-drachma coin (about four pennies), exactly the amount needed to pay the tax for both Jesus and himself!

By paying the Temple tax, Jesus demonstrated His loyalty to the Temple. But at the same time, the miraculous way in which He paid it showed that His authority as a teacher and prophet came from God. The priests and rulers should have known better than to argue anymore with Him. But they didn't.

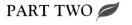

Seventy Times Seven

(Matthew 18:15-22; Luke 17:3, 4)

D OES your brother or your sister tease you a lot? Do you feel sometimes that you cannot take any more? What would Jesus do if He were in your place?

Let's ask the Prince of teachers and see what He says. Listen: "If your brother sins, rebuke him, and if he repents, forgive him. If he sins against you seven times in a day, and seven times comes back to you and says, 'I repent,' forgive him."

Seven times! you say. What a lot of times!

But no. When Peter came to Jesus and asked how many times he should forgive *his* brother, and whether seven times was the limit, Jesus said he was to go on forgiving him "seventy times seven" (RSV).

How many times is that? Four hundred and ninety! "Why," you say, "I couldn't keep count of all those times." Of course you couldn't! And Jesus knew that perfectly well when He said it. He doesn't keep count of the number of times He forgives us.

Four hundred and ninety times would mean once a day for more than a year! Have you ever tried forgiving anybody that many times? If not and you are feeling angry with somebody right now, get a notebook and pencil and start writing.

First, put down all the things this somebody has done to upset you. Next, write "forgiven" across the list. Then put a check mark beside that precious word every time you tell that person you forgive him when he annoys you again.

By the time you have made 20 or 30 check marks, that somebody may be your best friend. Try it and see.

Forgiving is part of God's better way, the way of love, which Jesus came from heaven to reveal to us. Forgiving some-

one over and over again—50 times, 100 times, 490 times—is love in action, love at its best and grandest, love reaching out to another heart with all its healing, winning power.

We can never hope to belong to Christ's kingdom of love if we do not know how to forgive people who do us wrong. He couldn't afford to let us in. We'd be having trouble with somebody in no time at all.

"Forgive us . . . as we also have forgiven," [1] we pray every time we say the Lord's Prayer. But how do we forgive? Just a little bit? Just once now and then? Just when we feel in the right mood? We wouldn't want God to forgive us like that.

No, Jesus wants us to be so full of His love that a forgiving spirit will come naturally. We will never be offended. No matter what anybody says or does to us, we will go on loving him or her just the same.

Jesus gave another illustration of how important He thinks this forgiving spirit is. He said that if we remember that someone is upset with us while we are on our way to church with a gift for God, we are to put away the gift until everything is straightened out with that person. "*First* go and be reconciled to your brother; then come and offer your gift," [2] He said.

To Jesus, a loving, forgiving spirit is much more important than money. He would far rather we make peace with an old enemy than give a big donation to a church building fund.

So we had better start forgiving right away. Think! Is there someone *you* should forgive today?

---

[1] Matthew 6:12.
[2] Matthew 5:24.

93

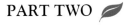

Mrs. Zebedee's Mistake

(Matthew 20:20-28)

THE BIBLE tells a good deal about the 12 disciples who followed Jesus, but it doesn't say much about their homes and families.

We know that Peter was married, for his mother-in-law once had a fever, and Jesus healed her. But that's about all, except for Mrs. Zebedee, the mother of James and John. She at least got her name in print if none of the others did. And that was because of a dreadful mistake she made.

Like all mothers, she was eager to see her children succeed. She wanted the best for her two precious boys, and there is nothing wrong about that. When she heard that James and John were going around with the great Teacher of Galilee, she was very glad, for she was sure He was a good man and would be a help to them.

As thousands flocked to Him and it seemed certain that He would become king of Israel someday, a bright idea came to her. The next time she found Jesus alone, she would

94

whisper a word in His ear about her sons. Perhaps He hadn't noticed how very suitable they were to hold high positions in His coming kingdom. They were really outstanding, much better qualified than the others, and He should know about it.

Her chance came at last. Finding Jesus alone, she went up to Him. James and John, looking a bit sheepish no doubt, were not far behind.

Kneeling, she told Jesus how much she thought of Him and His noble work, and how glad she was that He had chosen her two dear boys to be among His closest followers. She hoped they were giving Him all the help they should and, well, there was just one thing she would like to mention.

"What do you want?" asked Jesus kindly.

Looking around to make sure no one was listening, she whispered, eagerly, "Grant that one of these two sons of mine may sit at your right and the other at your left in your kingdom."

Jesus did not scold her. Perhaps He smiled at her, but there was sadness in His smile. He could see she did not understand anything about what His kingdom was really like or what it was going to cost those who believed in it.

Turning to James and John, He asked them whether they thought they could share His future, whatever it might be.

"Oh, yes," they said eagerly. "We can."

"You will . . . ," said Jesus, "but to sit at my right or left is not for me to grant. These places belong to those for whom they have been prepared by my Father."

A little later the whole story reached the ears of the other disciples. How, we don't know, but the best-kept secrets have a way of getting out.

The 10 were angry. To think that Mrs. Zebedee would do a thing like this! they muttered to each other. Pushing her own children ahead, that's what it was! Trying to cut the rest out! And they had worked just as hard, or harder, to set up the Master's kingdom.

Jesus knew what was going on. They couldn't have hidden their ugly thoughts from Him if they had tried. So He called them to Him and told them that it was time they all understood

96

what kind of kingdom they were working for.

In worldly kingdoms, He reminded them, rulers lord it over people, with big men bossing little men and demanding obedience. But this was not His way. In His kingdom, love, and love alone, ruled. Love was the key to promotion, and the chief offices were for those who served most humbly and unselfishly.

"Whoever wants to become great among you must be your servant," He said, "and whoever wants to be first must be your slave—just as the Son of Man did not come to be served, but to serve, and to give his life as a ransom for many."

Though many have forgotten what He said that day, this is still the way His kingdom is run—and will be, through all eternity.

Last Things Last

(Luke 10:38-42)

ARRIVING in the village of Bethany one day, Jesus knocked on the door of a humble home.

"Come in and welcome!" said the bright-eyed, vigorous woman who opened the door. It was Martha, and she was proud and glad that the famous Teacher of Galilee had come to her house to rest and eat.

"Mary!" I can hear her calling excitedly. "Mary! It's the Master. Hurry! Set the table! Fix the fire! Get that pot of beans boiling!"

At once the whole place was like a beehive, with Martha buzzing about at top speed doing all the things she thought should be done with such an important visitor in the house.

Soon a mixture of familiar sounds came from the kitchen. The clattering of pots and pans, the clink of dishes, the chop-chop-chop of a knife on wood, told that Martha was doing her best to give the Master the best meal she could.

Then after a long moment of silence, Martha shouted,

"Mary! Where are you? Mary! I need you to stir the soup! Mary!"

Quick footsteps followed, all the way from the kitchen to the living room. "Well, of all things!" cried Martha, as she caught sight of Mary sitting on the floor listening to Jesus.

Turning to her guest, she said, rather testily, "Don't you care that my sister has left me to do the work by myself? Tell her to help me!"

Jesus looked at her, smiling gently as usual. "Martha, Martha," He said tenderly, "you are worried and upset about many things, but only one thing is needed. Mary has chosen what is better, and it will not be taken away from her."

I don't think this means that Jesus did not appreciate all that Martha was doing. But He saw that Martha needed to learn a very important spiritual lesson.

You see, Jesus was there for just one little day; perhaps for one brief hour. Martha saw in this a chance to cook and to make her house all spick and span for their honored Guest, but Mary saw in it her one great opportunity to talk with the Prince of teachers. Here He was, right in her own home. For all she knew then, it would never happen again.

There would always be the house to clean, dishes to wash, and food to cook. But this day, this wonderful day, Jesus was here. And there were so many questions she wanted to ask Him about His teachings and His kingdom. There wouldn't be time to ask them all, but while He was here she would make the most of every precious moment in His presence.

This was "what is better," and what Mary had chosen to do. She could have chosen to sit on a kitchen stool and prepare vegetables, or mix a cheese omelet, but she chose instead to sit at Jesus' feet and learn from Him while she could.

Most of us need to make Mary's choice today. We are so much like Martha, rushing about at a terrible speed, clattering and banging our way through life, too busy to pray, too busy to read the Bible, too busy to go to church.

Of course we mustn't shirk our part of the humble, every-day duties. But let us try to put first things first and last things last, shall we?

And if we choose what is better, nobody will take it away from us. They couldn't. Not if we want it badly enough. 🖋

PART THREE

Stories of

the Prince of Storytellers

(Matthew 13:1-50; 18:23-35; 21:28-22:14; Mark 12:1-44;
Luke 8:4-15; 10:25-37; 14:16-15:32; 18:9-14; 20:9-19)

Seeds of Love

(Matthew 13:1-9, 18-23)

T HE PRINCE of teachers was also the Prince of storytellers. Some of His most precious lessons were given in true-to-life stories, which are sometimes called parables.

One day, as He was talking to a crowd of people on the shores of Galilee, He tried to make them see why they should listen carefully to what He was saying. He had come to show them a new way of life, but if they would not listen or try to understand, it wouldn't do them any good.

As He spoke a farmer was going about his lonely task in a nearby field. He was in full view of everyone listening to Jesus. This gave Jesus the idea for a story.

"A farmer went out to sow his seed," He said. "As he was scattering the seed, some fell along the path, and the birds came and ate it up. Some fell on rocky places. . . . But when the sun came up, the plants were scorched. . . . Other seed fell among thorns, which grew up and choked the plants. Still other seed fell on good soil, where it produced a crop—a hundred, sixty or

103

Seeing a sower in the fields Jesus taught them
a parable; "A sower went forth to sow," He
said; "and when he sowed, some seeds fell by
the way side and the fowls . . . devoured them."

thirty times what was sown."

The seed, He said later, was the word of God. We could call it the seed of love, for that was the word that Jesus had brought from God. "God loves you," He kept telling the people in various ways. "He loves you so much that He gave His only Son for you. In return He wants you to love Him and to love one another, so you may belong to His kingdom of love."

This was the heart of His message, the wonderful "seed" He was scattering. But it would help none of them if they did not understand and believe it. So they needed to listen, and think, and study, and decide.

Some in the crowd had hearts as hard as the path beside the field. He knew that. The moment a seed of love lodged in their minds, the devil would snatch it away.

Others would agree with His teaching and begin to put it into practice, but if someone laughed at them for following what Jesus taught, they would give it up. The "heat" would be too much for them.

Then there were those who would follow the better way for

a little while, but "the worries of this life and the deceitfulness of wealth" would choke their good resolutions as weeds choke good grain.

Some, however, not only would accept His message but would try to understand it. As they studied it, thought and prayed about it, they would catch a vision of God's wonderful plan to save them, and this seed of love would produce a great harvest of good.

Simple as the story was, not everybody in the crowd caught its meaning. But some did. Here and there a man or woman, a boy or girl, said softly, "He's talking about me!"

He was. And as He scattered His seeds of love He hoped that they would fall into many willing, friendly hearts where His love would take root, and produce a harvest "a hundred . . . times what was sown" to the glory of God.

No Weeds in Heaven

(Matthew 13:24-30, 36-43)

L ATER, in His great sermon by the lake, Jesus came back to His farmer-and-seed idea. This time, however, He had a new lesson to teach, so He told the story in a different way.

A farmer, He said, "sowed good seed in his field." The next night an enemy came and sowed weeds in it. When all the seeds began to grow, the farmer noticed the weeds and said, "An enemy did this."

His servants wanted to dig out the weeds right away, but the farmer wouldn't let them, in case they hurt the wheat too. "Let both grow together until the harvest," he said.

This was another very simple story, but it was full of deep meaning. Jesus explained it like this. The farmer who sowed the good seed is "the Son of Man"—Jesus Himself. "The field is the world, and the good seed stands for the sons of the kingdom. The weeds are the sons of the evil one, and the enemy who sows them is the devil. The harvest is the end of the age, and the harvesters are angels.

"As the weeds are pulled up and burned in the fire, so it will be at the end of the age. The Son of Man will send out his angels, and they will weed out of his kingdom everything that causes sin and all who do evil. They will throw them into the fiery furnace."

This was a warning that many standing there that day had not expected. They had begun to think that if God loved the world as much as Jesus said He did, He would surely overlook every kind of sin and let everybody, no matter how bad, into His kingdom.

No, said Jesus. That isn't so. God will gladly forgive all who repent of their sins and turn in love to Him. But where there's no repentance, there can be no forgiveness. For those who refuse God's love and keep on sinning, there is no hope. For them there is only the day of judgment, the harvest sifting, and the fire.

There will be no weeds in His kingdom.

The Good Samaritan

(Luke 10:25-37)

ONE DAY a lawyer came to Jesus and asked what seemed to be a very proper question. " 'Teacher,' he asked, 'what must I do to inherit eternal life?' "

Knowing that the man was only trying to start an argument, Jesus replied with another question, "What is written in the law?"

The lawyer answered, " 'Love the Lord your God with all your heart and with all your soul and with all your strength and with all your mind'; and, 'Love your neighbor as yourself.' "

"You have answered correctly," said Jesus. "Do this and you will live."

But the man was not satisfied. "Who is my neighbor?" he asked.

This gave Jesus the chance to teach this man a lesson he greatly needed. And He did it by telling one of His most famous stories, a story that has been told and retold thousands of times since then.

"A man was going down from Jerusalem to Jericho, when

he fell into the hands of robbers," said Jesus. These cutthroats beat up the lonely traveler, stole his clothes, and left him lying on the roadside half dead.

A priest happened to come by, but did not stop. He gave one glance at the injured man and "passed by on the other side." Next came a Levite. He at least took the trouble to go and look at the poor sufferer, but did nothing to help him. He too, "passed by on the other side."

Then came a Samaritan—one of those people the Jews hated so much. When he saw what had happened, he was filled with pity. Without a thought for himself, he decided to do what he could to help.

Kneeling beside the injured man, he cleaned his wounds the best he could and bandaged them. Then, very

carefully, the Samaritan placed the Jew on his own donkey and took him to the nearest inn. Here he got a room and food for him.

When he had to leave the next day, the Samaritan gave the innkeeper money. " 'Look after him,' he said, 'and when I return, I will reimburse you for any extra expense you may have.' "

"Now," said Jesus, looking straight at the lawyer, "which of these three do you think was a neighbor to the man who fell into the hands of robbers?"

"The one who had mercy on him," the lawyer replied.

"Go and do likewise," said Jesus.

Whether the lawyer took Jesus' advice we do not know. If he didn't, then he will never enjoy the eternal life he said he was looking for. For that rich reward is only for those whose hearts are filled to overflowing with love to God and man.

This love comes only from God, but He is more than willing to give it to us. All we have to do is ask Him, and He will make our hearts tender with compassion for the poor, the sick, the needy, and the oppressed. Our deeds of loving-kindness will show that we are good neighbors, good Samaritans, and true children of God.

Lost Sheep and Lost Coins

(Luke 15:1-10)

BECAUSE Jesus talked so much about the love of God and His willingness to forgive the worst sinners, He often had some of the worst characters around town in His audience.

Bad men and bad women came to listen to Him. Bad boys and bad girls did, too. Thieves, liars, cheats, rogues, ruffians, all the riffraff of society. And they came because He spoke the first word of hope they had ever heard.

Deep in their hearts many of them wanted to live a better life, but they didn't know how. They thought it wasn't possible. They felt trapped by their bad habits, bad friends, and their past evil deeds. There was no way out—until Jesus came. So they flocked to listen to Him.

To the Pharisees, teachers of the law, lawyers, and other "respectable" people, this was all very shocking. "This man welcomes sinners and eats with them!" they sneered, holding up their hands in horror.

But this was the finest thing they ever said about Jesus,

←— PAINTING BY HARRY ANDERSON

Jesus likened Himself to a faithful shepherd who, although he had ninety-nine sheep safe in the fold, would go out into the mountains to find the one lost sheep that had gone astray.

though they didn't mean it that way. The chief glory of Jesus is that He does welcome sinners. He has been welcoming them for a long time now and still welcomes them. Even the worst sinners may be sure of acceptance. If you feel you are a sinner, He will welcome you right now.

How do I know? Because of what He said to the teachers of the law and the Pharisees that day. "If you had 100 sheep and lost one of them, what would you do?" He asked them. "Forget it? No. You would leave the 99 and go after that one lost sheep and search till you found it. Then you would put it on your shoulder and bring it home, calling to your friends and neighbors, 'Rejoice with me; I have found my lost sheep.' "

Every man there knew he would do just that. Some perhaps had already done it, searching patiently for hours, traveling many miles, climbing dangerous mountain trails, risking death on steep cliffs, plodding on through snow and hail and thunderstorm, all for one lost sheep.

For one lost man, one lost boy, one lost girl, however, they wouldn't lift a finger. But God cares more for the lost man, the lost boy, the lost girl, than for any lost sheep.

"I tell you . . . ," said Jesus very earnestly, "there will be more rejoicing in heaven over one sinner who repents than over ninety-nine righteous persons who do not need to repent."

Then He turned to the women and reminded them of what they do when they lose one little coin. "Though you have nine coins left in your purse, you will light a lamp and sweep the house and search

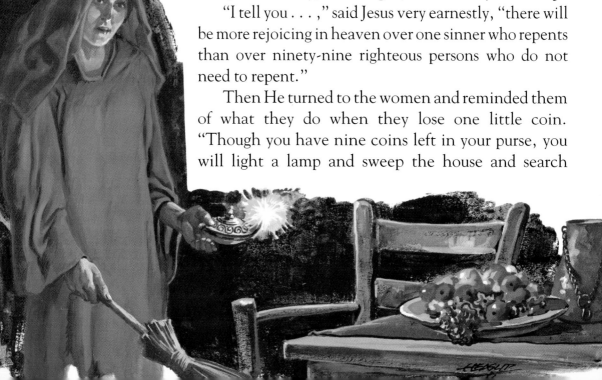

carefully till you find it. And when you have found it, you
will call your friends and neighbors and say, 'Rejoice with
me; I have found my lost coin.' Isn't that so?"

I can see them smiling and nodding their heads. That
was just what they would do. How well He understood
them!

"In the same way . . . ," said Jesus, "there is rejoicing in
the presence of the angels of God over one sinner who
repents."

So Jesus became known as the sinners' Friend. He took their
part and gave them hope. Even the worst of them, who had
wandered the farthest from the fold, now knew that Somebody
cared for them, and cared enough to come after them and
search for them. And how wonderful it was to know that the
angels also cared, and all heaven would ring with joy over every
sinner who repented!

Here was love at work again. Love, like a mighty magnet,
pulling and tugging at human hearts, breaking the hold of sin
and Satan and bringing them home to God.

Lost Boy Found

(Luke 15:11-32)

OF ALL the stories Jesus told, the most touching and beautiful is the one about the runaway boy who came home. It is best known as the story of the Prodigal Son.

"There was a man," said Jesus, "who had two sons." Both lived on their father's ranch, both were well off, and both were equally loved.

But the younger son was restless. He was tired of being told what to do and what not to do. He wanted to be free to do as he pleased. Most of all, he wanted to enjoy the pleasures of city life he had heard about.

One day he went to his father and asked for the share of the property that would come to him when his father died. Of course, he had no right to ask for this now, but his father who loved him dearly, gave it to him. Feeling very rich and happy, the boy rode away to "a distant country" he had wanted so long to see.

For a while he had a marvelous time. Because of his great

riches he made many friends. Between them they spent the money as fast as they could.

Then one day the young man discovered that all of his money was gone. He was poor, without a penny left. His friends weren't interested in him anymore, since his money was gone, so they all left him.

About this time a "severe famine" struck the "whole country." Food supplies ran short. Soon everybody was starving. The young man tried to find work, but the only job he could get was caring for pigs. He was so hungry that he was tempted to eat the pigs' food.

One day as he sat alone with the animals, "he came to his senses." He thought about all his father's servants and how well they ate all the time. "They have more than enough food, and here I sit starving to death!" he said to himself.

Suddenly he made up his mind. "I will set out and go back to my father and say to him: Father, I have sinned against heaven and against you. I am no longer worthy to be called your son; make me like one of your hired men."

117

Leaving the pigs, he set off for home. It was a long, long journey, for he had to walk all the way, and he was almost worn out with hunger and fatigue. Every weary mile he wondered what his father would say to him. Perhaps he would refuse even to see him.

But he did not need to worry, for every day since he had left home his father had been looking for him, hoping he would return. And now, when the son was still "a long way off," the father saw him and recognized him, despite his torn clothes, his sagging shoulders, his untidy beard.

Gone were the horses, the fine clothes, and the money-bags the son took with him when he left home but what did the father care? His boy had come back at last! With a cry of joy he ran toward him, never stopping until his arms were wrapped around his son.

"Father," the boy cried, looking up into the tear-stained face above him, "Father, I have sinned against heaven and against you. I am no longer worthy to be called your son—"

He got no further. By this time several servants had come running up. "Bring the best robe, and put it on him," ordered the father, now radiantly happy. "Put a ring on his finger and sandals on his feet. Bring the fattened calf and kill it. Let's have a feast and celebrate. For this son of mine was dead and is alive again; he was lost and is found."

This was how Jesus tried to tell the poor sinners how glad God would be if only they too would come back

119

← PAINTING BY HARRY ANDERSON

The prodigal son had spent his money and his health in wickedness and dissipation, but one day among the swine he realized his sinfulness and resolved to return to his father's house.

to Him. But this was not the end of the story.

When the older son heard that his brother had been given such a welcome, even though he had behaved so badly and wasted so much money, he was very angry. " 'All these years I've been slaving for you and never disobeyed your orders. Yet you never gave me even a young goat so I could celebrate with my friends. But when this son of yours who has squandered your property with prostitutes comes home, you kill the fattened calf for him!'

" 'My son,' the father said, 'you are always with me, and everything I have is yours. But we had to celebrate and be glad, because this brother of yours was dead and is alive again; he was lost and is found.' "

The brother who stayed at home, who never got into trouble, should have been just as happy about the bad boy's return as his father was. We all should rejoice, as God does, over every sinner who comes back to Him. 🖋

Improper Wedding Clothes

(Matthew 22:1-14)

ONCE upon a time, said Jesus, there was a king who planned a wedding banquet for his son. He sent out invitations to all the important people in his kingdom and expected that they would be glad and honored to come.

But they didn't come. One after another sent word to say, "Sorry, but I won't be there."

So the king sent his servants to invite the people personally and urge them to change their minds, but still they would not come. Some kings would have been very angry at being treated like this, but this one was kind and patient. He decided to give them all one more chance.

As the wedding day drew near he sent out other servants to say to those who had been invited, "Everything is ready; the food is all prepared. Come! Do come!"

But again they refused. In fact, they acted as though they didn't care about the wedding at all. One went off to his farm, another to his place of business. Some even seized the king's servants, beat them up, and killed them.

This was too much for the king. Kind and good though he was, he would not stand for this. So he ordered his soldiers to destroy the murderers and burn up their city.

But still there were no guests at the wedding. So now the king called his servants and said to them, "The wedding banquet is ready, but those I invited did not deserve to come. Go to the street corners and invite to the banquet anyone you find."

Off they went to do as they were told. "How would you like to come to the palace tonight?" they asked a beggar on the roadside.

"What, me?" said the poor man, unable to believe his ears.

"Yes, you! Come along. You will be welcome. The king has asked for you. Just make sure you wear the wedding clothes."

So they invited everybody they met, "both good and bad." Soon hundreds of poor, needy people were hurrying

toward the king's palace from all directions.

When everyone arrived at the wedding hall, the king came in to greet them. I can imagine everybody stood and cheered, for they were so glad to be there.

Suddenly, however, there was silence. Something was wrong. The king walked up to one of the guests. " 'Friend,' he asked, 'how did you get in here without wedding clothes?' "

Frightened, the man said nothing. Then, to everybody's surprise, the king gave orders that he be tied hand and foot and carried outside.

What was the meaning of this story about a king and his banquet? Why did Jesus tell it?

The good, kind king, of course, was God, and his son was Jesus. The invited guests were the leaders of Israel. The king's servants were the prophets God had sent times without number, urging the leaders of Israel to repent and return to Him.

What about the people who were found on the streets, the

poor and needy, the good and bad? Who were they? They were the men and women, the boys and girls, right in front of Jesus at the time—and everybody like them from that day to this. He told the story for them, to let them know they were welcome, many times welcome, in His Father's kingdom.

They might be the poorest of the poor. They might never have been to school. They might never have had a nice home or a single chance in life. But if they accepted God's loving invitation, they could share the best He had to offer. The wedding banquet of the King of heaven was wide open to them.

There was just one condition. They must put on "wedding clothes." But where would poor people find such expensive robes? They certainly could not afford to buy them. The king would have to provide them himself.

What kind of special clothes was Jesus talking about? They must be spotlessly clean and very, very beautiful.

Long before Jesus told this story, the prophet Isaiah had written about God wanting to clothe His people in robes of goodness and salvation.* These are the glorious garments that must be wrapped about all who plan to attend His wedding, and God will gladly give them to us.

And that means you and me.

---

¹ See Isaiah 61:10.

Inexcusable Excuses

(Luke 14:15-24)

JESUS told another story very much like the one about the royal wedding. Only this one was about a big feast. "A certain man," He said, "was preparing a great banquet and invited many guests."

At great expense this man had his servants prepare the hall where the dinner was to be held. The long white tables gleamed with sparkling silver and groaned under all the good food piled on them. Bright lights and soft music made the scene inviting. Only the guests were missing.

They had been invited, but they had not come. They were late. So the man sent his servant to say to them, "Come, for everything is now ready."

But they weren't even interested. Instead, they all began to make excuses. One said, "I have just bought a field, and I must go and see it. Please excuse me."

Another invited guest said, "I have just bought five yoke of oxen, and I'm on my way to try them out. Please excuse me."

125

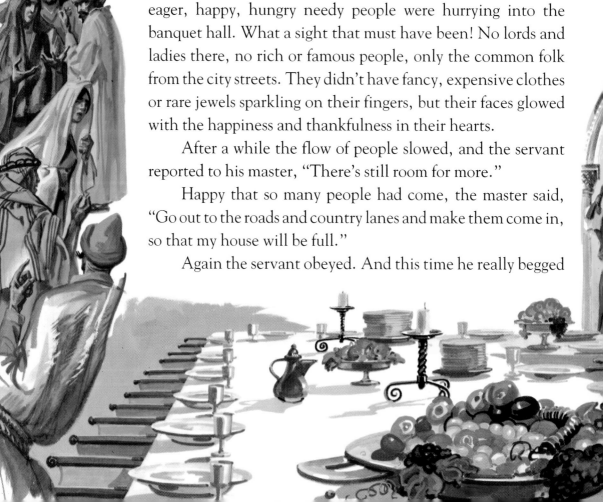

A third said, "I just got married so I can't come."

They didn't care about the banquet. Their minds were on other things. The fact that the good man had gone to so much trouble and expense to make them happy didn't mean a thing to them.

Soon the servant returned to his master and told him what had happened. The good man was very hurt, as you or I would have been. Then he took one look at the big empty hall, with all those long tables covered with food, and said to his servant, "Go out quickly into the streets and alleys of the town and bring in the poor, the crippled, the blind and the lame."

The servant did as he was told, and soon hundreds of eager, happy, hungry needy people were hurrying into the banquet hall. What a sight that must have been! No lords and ladies there, no rich or famous people, only the common folk from the city streets. They didn't have fancy, expensive clothes or rare jewels sparkling on their fingers, but their faces glowed with the happiness and thankfulness in their hearts.

After a while the flow of people slowed, and the servant reported to his master, "There's still room for more."

Happy that so many people had come, the master said, "Go out to the roads and country lanes and make them come in, so that my house will be full."

Again the servant obeyed. And this time he really begged

the people to come. "Please come!" he pleaded. "The banquet is ready, and the hall is nearly full."

In this story Jesus revealed again the wonderful love of God for this world. He has gone to great pains to prepare for our happiness. He has prepared a marvelous feast of good things and has invited everybody to share it. But some don't care. They are too busy with plans of their own.

I have called this story the story of the inexcusable excuses. And we must be careful that we too don't find reasons for not doing God's will.

Maybe you have heard a boy say, "I don't want to go to church today; I've promised my friends I'd play ball with them."

Or, perhaps you've heard a girl say, "Let's not have worship this evening; there's a program on television we simply mustn't miss."

Or you yourself may have said, "I won't bother to say my prayers tonight; I'm too tired."

These are all excuses for not doing what you know God wants you to do. And they are inexcusable excuses; for there never can be any good excuse for saying, "I don't care what's right"; "I don't care what God says"; or "I don't care whether or not He's disappointed in me."

Such excuses are dangerous. They will lead you to make other excuses later on. And not only could they keep you from the banquet of good things God has prepared for you, they could keep you out of heaven.

Meanest Man on Earth

(Matthew 18:23-35)

J UST to show how mean some people can be, Jesus told this story about a man who had been forgiven a very large debt.

A certain king, He said, decided to check up on the accounts of his servants. He discovered that one of them owed him 10,000 talents of silver—an enormous sum of money, equal to many millions of dollars.

So he sent for the man and asked him how much he could pay on his debt.

"Nothing," said the man. "I don't have a penny." He had spent it all.

So the king gave orders that the man, his wife, and his children should be sold as slaves "to repay the debt."

At this the man fell on his knees and begged the king for mercy. If only he could have more time, he said, he would pay the debt. " 'Be patient with me,' he begged, 'and I will pay back everything.' "

128

The king felt sorry for the poor man, so he canceled the entire huge debt and set him free.

How surprised and happy the man must have been! But as he walked out of the gate he ran into a friend who owed *him* some money. It wasn't much. Just 100 denarii, worth only a few dollars. But he made up his mind that he wanted it returned now.

"When are you going to pay that debt?" he asked.

"Sorry, but I can't pay it," said his friend. "I simply don't have the money."

"Pay back what you owe me!" cried the man, seizing the other by the throat.

"I can't! I can't!" gasped the poor debtor.

"All right, then," snarled the one who had just been forgiven 10,000 talents, "we'll see about that. It's prison for you."

"Be patient with me," cried the other man, "and I will pay you back."

You would think that the first man would have recognized those words. They were his own plea for mercy to the king. But he didn't. Instead, he hurried his friend off to prison and said he could stay there until he had paid the whole debt.

Fortunately somebody saw what happened and told the king about it. The king couldn't believe that anyone could be so mean. So he sent for the man and told him what he thought of him.

" 'You wicked servant,' he said, 'I canceled all that debt of

8-9

yours because you begged me to. Shouldn't you have had mercy on your fellow servant just as I had on you?' "

Then he gave orders that this meanest of men should be put in prison and kept there until he had paid all the 10,000 talents he had owed.

When the story ended, Jesus looked solemnly at the people about Him. "This is how my heavenly Father will treat each of you," He said, "unless you forgive your brother from your heart."

It was a great lesson in forgiveness. In His great mercy God is willing to forgive us all our sins, to blot them out and forget them. He is willing to treat us as though we had never done anything wrong. But He wants us to forgive others in the same way, *from our hearts.*

The man who was forgiven a 10,000-talent debt and then put his friend in jail because he couldn't pay a hundred denarii was certainly a mean, cruel man. But was he any meaner than someone today who, having been forgiven all his sins by God, still holds a grudge in his heart toward someone who has wronged him or her?

How is it with you? Have you forgiven everybody who has hurt you or annoyed you, as God has forgiven you? If a competition were held to find the meanest person on earth today—the meanest man, the meanest woman, the meanest boy or girl—where would you stand?

Two Boys and Their Dad

(Matthew 21:28-32)

ANOTHER story Jesus told was about two boys and a job their father wanted them to do.

One day this father came to one of his sons and said to him, "I want you to work in the vineyard today."

"I won't!" said the boy, and he walked off in a huff. He hated working in the vineyard, and anyway there were lots of other things he would rather do. But as he thought things over, he began to feel sorry for the way he had spoken to his father.

"Poor old Dad!" he may have said to himself, "I shouldn't have become angry with him. He certainly has a lot to do around here. Why didn't I offer to help him?" The boy decided to go to the vineyard after all, and off he went.

The other son was different. When his father came to him and said, "I want you to work in the vineyard today, son," he answered, "Certainly, Dad. I'll go there right away." But he never went. In fact, he had no intention of going.

No sooner was his father out of sight than he went fishing,

or hunting, or maybe he just played with the neighbor boys. Anyway, he never turned up at the vineyard.

"Which of these two boys," asked Jesus, "obeyed his father? The one who said No and went, or the one who said Yes and didn't go?"

"The first," cried everybody.

"Of course," said Jesus.

Then He pointed out the lesson of His story. It is much better in God's sight to repent and begin to live right than to pretend to do right and still keep on in one's old, bad ways.

"Some of you," He said, "went to hear John the Baptist. He preached righteousness and told you to repent. Some of you said you would, but you didn't. It was all a show. But a lot of poor sinners did repent. They may have been the worst people

132

in the world, but they'll go into heaven before those who just pretend to be good."

In telling this story, Jesus tried again to help the people see the importance of true repentance. He wanted them to understand that if they hoped to enter heaven and belong to His kingdom of love, they had to turn from their wicked ways and do the will of God.

It would not be enough for them just to *say* they were going to repent and be good. They would have to *mean* it in their hearts. To say "I repent" and go on living the same old sinful life would be acting a lie—just as the boy did who said he would work in the vineyard and never went near it.

There's a lesson in this story for us, too. It's very easy today to make a show of being a follower of Jesus. Lots of people claim to be Christians who are not really Christians at

133

all. They say they are on their way to heaven because it sounds nice, but they much prefer to go on enjoying themselves in this old world.

People who act like this will never get to heaven. They just don't belong there. The kingdom of God is not only a kingdom of love but a kingdom of honesty, sincerity, purity, goodness, truth. And if we want to belong to that kingdom, we'll have to fit into God's plans for it.

The only way we can do that is to follow the example of the first boy in the story—the one who repented. He said, "I won't," but on second thought he turned around and said, "I will."

We must do the same.

And it doesn't matter how bad we may have been, or how mean, how rude, how obstinate. If we are willing to change, to repent, to turn about-face and do God's will, He will receive us with gladness and forgive all our sins.

Maybe sometime lately you have said "I won't" to God. "I won't" obey His commandments, or "I won't" go where He asks me, or "I won't" belong to His church, or "I won't" give my heart to Him.

If so, think it over. Remember how dearly He loves you. "As a father," * the Bible says. Then why not turn to Him at this very moment? Just say, "I'm sorry, Lord; I'm coming after all. I'll do as You say." ✐

---

* Psalm 103:13.

135

← PAINTING BY RUSSELL HARLAN

God loves every boy and girl who listens to the counsel of his Christian parents, and when tempted to do wrong makes the decision that no matter what comes he will serve the Lord.

Murder in a Vineyard

(Matthew 21:33-46)

ID JESUS actually tell a murder story? He surely did.

There was once a wealthy landowner, He said, who planted a beautiful vineyard. He thought so much of it that he couldn't do enough for it. Carefully he prepared the soil and set out the precious vines. Then he built a tower for the watchmen and a winepress to crush the grapes when they were ripe.

Finally he put a wall all around the vineyard to protect it from enemies. When all this was done, he left the place in the care of tenants he thought he could trust and went away to another country.

After a long time the vines became heavy with grapes, and the owner sent his servants to get the fruit. But when the tenants saw the owner's servants coming, "they beat one, killed another, and stoned a third."

That was the first murder in the vineyard, but not the last. When the householder sent another group of servants

136

to gather the fruit, these also were stoned and killed.

At last the householder said to himself, "I'll send my son. They will surely respect him."

But they didn't. Instead, the tenants said among themselves, "This is the heir. Come, let's kill him and take his inheritance." So they murdered the son too.

At this point Jesus asked His listeners what they thought the owner of the vineyard would do to these cruel and unworthy tenants.

" 'He will bring those wretches to a wretched end,' they replied, 'and he will rent the vineyard to other tenants, who will give him his share of the crop.' "

Jesus agreed they were right. Then, looking straight at some of the priests and Pharisees who were listening to Him, He said, "The kingdom of God will be taken away from you and given to a people who will produce its fruit."

Now the meaning of this story became plain. The Bible says that these priests and Pharisees "knew He was talking about them."

The vineyard, of course, was the nation of Israel, planted by God Himself. Tenderly He had cared for it and protected it, expecting a rich harvest of the finest fruit. But when He had sent His prophets to gather it, they had been treated as enemies by the religious leaders who should have welcomed them. Many had been beaten,

stoned, and killed. So at last
God decided to send His Son. And they
were about to kill Him too.

Of course, when Jesus told this story, this last awful
thing was still in the future. But the fact that He mentioned it
shows that He knew it was going to happen.

What about the next tenants who were given an opportunity to look after the vineyard? These were His disciples—
not only those who were with Him then but all who would
believe in Him and love Him and work for Him in years to
come. He saw them nurturing the good fruits of love, truth,
and goodness in the lives of countless thousands of others
until the final harvest of the vineyard was ripe.

All these dear ones would make up the new nation to
whom the kingdom of God would be given. And
this nation, not belonging to any one race
or people but gathered from the world
out of "every nation, tribe, people and
language," * would be *His*

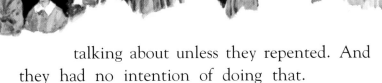

nation over which He would reign forever and ever. Eden would be restored, and the purposes of God would be completed.

This story, with all its wonderful meaning, angered the priests and Pharisees who heard it. They saw plainly that they could have no part in this kingdom Jesus was talking about unless they repented. And they had no intention of doing that.

They became so enraged with Him they would have put Him in prison then and there had they dared. But they didn't dare. The Bible says, "They were afraid of the crowd because the people held that he was a prophet."

---

* Revelation 7:9.

Praying and Giving

(Luke 18:9-14; 21:1-4)

JESUS was always looking for new stories with great lessons, and more often than not He found them in the lives of people He met and mixed with day after day.

Once while in the Temple He saw two men at prayer. One was a Pharisee, and the other was a tax collector. The Pharisee was standing where everybody could see and hear him and the other man was back in a corner.

In a loud voice the Pharisee was telling God about himself. "God," he cried, "I thank you that I am not like other men — robbers, evildoers, adulterers — or even like this tax collector. I fast twice a week and give a tenth of all I get."

Then the tax collector, his hands beating his chest, his head bowed in sorrow, his voice so low it could scarcely be heard, said this brief and humble prayer. "God, have mercy on me, a sinner."

When Jesus told this story to His disciples some time later, He added, "I tell you that this man [meaning the tax collector], rather than the other, went home justified before God."

141

The Pharisees liked to appear very pious by making long prayers in public places, but Jesus loved the humble publican more who cried, "God be merciful to me a sinner."

The Pharisee was merely trying to advertise his own good deeds, and God doesn't listen to prayers like that. But when someone whispers, "God, have mercy on me, a sinner," every word is heard in heaven.

If you want to talk to God sometime, don't tell Him how good you are or how many kind deeds you have done. Just tell Him how much you need His help.

Another time when Jesus was in the Temple, He saw something very beautiful happen—something that has been a blessing to millions ever since.

He was sitting quietly near the treasury, watching the people put in their gifts of money. Many rich people came by and gave large sums. Then a poor widow walked slowly up to the box and put in two very small copper coins, worth less than a penny.

"Look at the woman who just passed by the offering box,"

Jesus said to His disciples who were not far away. "This poor widow has put in more than all the others. All these people gave their gifts out of their wealth; but she out of her poverty put in all she had to live on."

The widow did not know Jesus was watching her, but He was. And He knew by the look on her face and the prayer on her lips that her gift was from her heart and that it was everything she had.

I like to think that she was rewarded that very day and angels were sent to take care of her needs. But whatever happened to her, I know that when Jesus said, "She gave more than all the others," it was true not only that day, but has been true ever since.

In real value—as God values gifts—her two very small copper coins were worth far, far more than all the gold and silver dropped carelessly into the box by the rich people ahead

of her. And when all the money ever given to God is finally added up, it may well be found that this poor widow's offering will top the list.

When the widow is shown the total, I am sure she will exclaim, "There's been a mistake. I never gave all that!"

But Jesus will say to her, "Oh, but you did. All this was given because of what you gave."

How true! For nearly 2,000 years the story of this widow's sacrifice has been told and told again. It has gone around the world and echoed down the centuries. It has touched hearts and opened purses and made people give their best for the Master more times than anyone could ever count.

Of course, it wasn't the amount of the gift that really mattered but the spirit in which the widow gave it. Her heart must have been God's already before she gave her money. The two little coins were just the final proof that "all she had" was His.

That is the way we should give to God—with all our hearts. This is the only kind of giving that will be of much help in building His kingdom of love.

JIM PAXTON

PART FOUR

Stories of

the Prince of Prophets

(Matthew 24:1-25:46; Mark 13:1-37;
Luke 17:21-37; 19:12-27; 21:1-36; John 13:36-14:3)

Homes for the Homeless

(Matthew 19:27-29; John 13:33-14:3)

JESUS was not only the Prince of healers, the Prince of teachers, and the Prince of storytellers, but He was also the Prince of prophets. He could see into the future. He knew what was going to happen in the days ahead.

Many prophets, including Moses, Samuel, Isaiah, Jeremiah, and Daniel, had spoken to Israel before Jesus came. But Jesus was the greatest of them all. He talked about things to come as though He knew all about them.

And there was so much the disciples wanted to know about the future! Like you and me, they wanted to see tomorrow as clearly as today.

Once Peter said to Jesus, "We have left everything to follow you! What then will there be for us?"

Jesus had just told His disciples how hard it is for rich people to enter His kingdom; so Peter wanted to know what reward there was for those who had given up everything, as he and his friends had done. He was thinking of their boats, their fishing nets, their little homes. They had left everything for

147

One of the last lessons Jesus taught His disciples was that in heaven there would be no homeless families, for He was going there to prepare mansions for all who loved God.

Jesus. Now they were poor, with sometimes not even a place to sleep except on the open hillside.

Was it always going to be like this? Would they never have a home again?

For a moment, to cheer them up, Jesus let them look ahead. "I tell you the truth," He said, "at the renewal of all things, when the Son of Man sits on his glorious throne, you who have followed me will also sit on twelve thrones, judging the twelve tribes of Israel. And everyone who has left houses or brothers or sisters or father or mother or children or fields for my sake will receive a hundred times as much and will inherit eternal life."

I can see Peter, James, John, and the rest of them smiling at each other as Jesus made this promise. To think that they, just humble folk from Galilee, would be the chief judges of Israel! How wonderful! Yes! And at last they would all have nice houses to live in. Never again would they have to wander from place to place, hungry, thirsty, and homeless.

But there was something else they wanted to know. For some time now Jesus had been dropping hints that He wouldn't be with them much longer.

148

"My children," He said to them once, very tenderly, "I will be with you only a little longer. . . . Where I am going, you cannot come."

Peter was worried. An awful lonesomeness clutched at his heart. "Lord, where are You going?" he asked.

"Where I am going, you cannot follow now," said Jesus, "but you will follow later."

"Why can't I follow You now?" asked Peter. He was puzzled. So were the rest of the disciples. They could not bring themselves to believe that soon their beloved Master would leave them. And if He did, what would happen to all His promises of houses and friends and loved ones and everlasting life?

Perhaps, they thought, He was planning to go to Greece or Italy and would soon be back again. Some of the Jews even asked, "Where does this man intend to go that we cannot find him? Will he go where our people live scattered among the Greeks, and teach the Greeks?" *

But Jesus didn't mean that. He was going much farther away than Athens or Rome. He was going back to heaven, where He had been before He had come to this earth.

"Do not let your hearts be troubled," He said to them in words that will live forever. "Trust in God; trust also in me. In my Father's house are many rooms; if it were not so, I would have told you. I am going there to prepare a place for you. And if I go and prepare a place for you, I will come back and take you to be with me that you also may be where I am going."

He could not have spoken more plainly. He was going far away—to His Father's house.

Maybe He was looking up at the stars as He spoke. Somewhere at the heart and hub of this great shining universe He would meet the One who had sent Him, the One He so dearly loved.

But no matter how far He went or how long He stayed away, He would never forget His disciples. No, indeed. Instead He would prepare a place for them and make it lovelier each passing day.

There would be lots of room for all of them. Among the 1,000 billion orbs He had created, there were many places— enough for all who loved Him. There would be a place for Peter, another for James, and another for John. And there would be one each for all of His faithful followers. Not one would be homeless anymore.

---

* John 7:35.

Space Flight Promised

(John 14:3; 1 Thessalonians 4:16, 17; Revelation 7:14-17)

HOW WOULD the disciples ever enjoy the lovely homes Jesus had promised them?

"I will come back," He assured them, "and take you to be with me that you also may be where I am going."

This was a solemn promise, and we may be certain He will keep it. True, He has not come back yet. He is still in His Father's house, but someday He will return for His own. And that means a space flight for all of His faithful followers.

It's marvelous to think about; but some 2,000 years ago, long before all the voyages to the moon, long before little boys were buying space helmets and little girls were dreaming of trips to Mars and Venus, Jesus told His disciples they would someday journey through the universe. When He comes back to this earth again, He will gather all His people to Himself and lead them out through "the wild blue yonder" to His Father's house.

Peter, James, and John will not be the only ones who will enjoy this rare privilege. All who have loved Jesus and been loyal to Him will be able to go along too.

151

SPACE FLIGHT PROMISED

The apostle Paul was very clear about this. When he wrote to the Christians at Thessalonica, he said, "The Lord Himself will come down from heaven with a loud command, with the voice of the archangel and with the trumpet call of God, and the dead in Christ will rise first. After that, we who are still alive and are left will be caught up together with them in the clouds to meet the Lord in the air. And so we will be with the Lord forever."

Imagine it! "Caught up together . . . in the clouds to meet the Lord in the air"! How very, very thrilling! Sailing out toward the moon! Flying from planet to planet! Soaring off to the stars! It seems impossible, but it must be true, for Jesus has promised it.

The apostle John thought this promise was so wonderful that he couldn't get it out of his mind. One day God gave him a

HERBERT RUDEEN, ARTIST

vision of the followers of Jesus when at last they get to heaven. He saw them all wearing white robes, and an angel said to him, "These are they who have come out of the great tribulation; they have washed their robes and made them white in the blood of the Lamb. Therefore they are before the throne of God and serve Him day and night in His temple. . . . Never again will they hunger; never again will they thirst. The sun will not beat upon them, nor any scorching heat.

"For the Lamb at the center of the throne will be their shepherd; he will lead them to springs of living water. And God will wipe away every tear from their eyes."

There it is again, the same glorious picture of Jesus leading His redeemed through His Father's house, where there are homes for all, and no one is ever hungry, or thirsty, or lonesome anymore.

Is it too good to be true, too wonderful to happen?

No. Many people have taken somewhat short trips through space. But the greatest Scientist and Space Engineer of all has known all about space travel from the beginning. The Prince of prophets saw it coming long, long ago.

He thought of it first. He knows the secret of how to travel through the universe on a far grander scale than we can imagine; and someday He plans to share this secret with all who love Him.

Jesus Unveils the Future

(Matthew 24:1-13)

A S THE disciples talked among themselves about the wonderful things Jesus had told them they longed to know more about the future.

If He was going to leave them, what would happen to them after He was gone? How long would He be away? When would this present world end and *His* world, His beautiful kingdom of love, begin?

At last they found a chance to ask Him. One day, while looking at the massive walls of the Temple, Jesus startled them all by saying, "Do you see all these things? . . . I tell you the truth, not one stone here will be left on another; every one will be thrown down."

The disciples could hardly believe their ears. The Temple destroyed! How could that ever happen? Such a beautiful building too, and so costly! Who would ever want to wreck it? Perhaps Jesus meant He was going to throw it down Himself when He came to set up His kingdom. Or would it be the work of enemies? They made up their minds to find out.

155

Back on the Mount of Olives, where the little group often met, they asked Him. " 'Tell us,' they said, 'when will this happen, and what will be the sign of your coming and of the end of the age?' "

Jesus told them. Drawing back the curtain that hides the future, He let them look into the years ahead.

It was not a bit as they had expected. I wouldn't be surprised if afterward they wished they hadn't asked Him. Sometimes it's better not to know the future, but to leave it in the hands of God.

First, Jesus warned them always to watch out for false christs. He said that after He had gone away one man after another would arise and say, "I am the Christ," and claim to have come back just as Jesus promised He would do.

As for the promised kingdom, that would not be set up for a long time yet. "You will hear of wars and rumors of wars," He said. "Nation will rise against nation, and kingdom against kingdom. There will be famines and earthquakes in various places."

All these terrible things would just be "the beginning of birth pains." Far worse troubles would come to the disciples. They would be cruelly treated. Enemies would put them in prison and kill them.

"You will be hated by all nations because of me," said Jesus.

Because of all this suffering, many who claim to be His followers "will turn away from the faith and will betray and hate each other." Wickedness would increase and love grow cold. Some faithful ones, however, would never give up. They would stand firm to the end and be saved.

Jesus now began to talk about Jerusalem, which at this moment lay peacefully below them. Great trouble would come to this city, He said, and soon. A foreign

LARS JUSTINEN

army would utterly destroy it.

The disciples could save themselves from this disaster by watching for a certain sign. The moment they saw the city surrounded by soldiers, they were to run to a place of safety. They must not delay a moment, not even to pick up a single treasure. If they were working in a field, they must not go home to get their clothes. If they ran for dear life, they would have just enough time to escape.

Then Jesus said a strange thing. He told them to pray that they wouldn't have to escape in the winter or on the Sabbath day.

On that quiet, peaceful afternoon on the Mount of Olives, it must have been hard for the disciples to imagine the scenes Jesus was talking about. Their lives in dear old Galilee had been so peaceful. They had never seen a great city besieged by armies. And the very idea of their holy city being destroyed was frightening to them. Would it really happen?

Later they told other disciples what Jesus had said, and the

news spread far and wide. Many believers began to pray that their flight would not be on the Sabbath or in the winter.

Some must have wondered how they would be able to escape if Jerusalem were surrounded by an army. It did seem strange, come to think of it. But they went on believing that Jesus couldn't have made a mistake.

Of course He hadn't. About 40 years later Jerusalem was surrounded by Roman soldiers. Recognizing the promised sign, the Christians in the city prepared to escape. Then, just as they were wondering how they would get through the enemy lines, the Romans mysteriously withdrew. Every follower of Jesus who believed His warning got away. Then the Romans returned and destroyed the city.

How wonderful that Jesus had known all this so long before it happened! But, of course, He was the Prince of prophets.

Back on that lonely hillside He now began to tell His disciples about other things that would happen hundreds of years ahead—right on down to the end of time. 🖋

Signs of His Coming

(Matthew 24:21-33; Luke 21:24-36)

L OOKING far into the future, Jesus told His disciples about a terrible time of trouble that would come to all who loved Him. "There will be great distress," He said, "unequaled from the beginning of the world until now—and never to be equaled again."

The prophet Daniel had written about a terrible time when the little horn on the head of the fourth beast would "oppress his saints." * Jesus knew this story well. He was the One who had sent Gabriel to tell Daniel about it.

Now, as He retold it to His disciples, He was sad for His "elect"—His dear people who would suffer so much. Not only would the new little band of believers suffer hardships and trials and death soon after He was gone, but trouble and persecution would follow them down through to the end of time. There would be an especially difficult time of trouble just before Jesus came again.

During those days of sorrow and suffering, more and more frauds would claim to be Christ, returning from heaven. The

people would be so tired and eager for the trouble to end that many would be deceived.

False christs and false prophets would appear, performing "great signs and miracles." But, said Jesus, don't follow them. "If anyone says to you, 'Look, here is the Christ!' or, 'There he is!' do not believe it."

If they say, Look! He is in the desert, don't go to look for Him there.

If they say, Look! He is in some secret room, don't believe it. He won't be there either.

They were to watch for certain great events, each one so big and important that no deceiver could imitate it. The first would be in the sky, which God would use as a huge advertising sign.

"There will be signs in the sun, moon and stars," said Jesus. "The sun will be darkened, and the moon will not give its light;

8-11

161

the stars will fall from the sky."

The next signs would be on the earth. "On the earth, nations will be in anguish and perplexity at the roaring and tossing of the sea. Men will faint from terror, apprehensive of what is coming on the world, for the heavenly bodies will be shaken."

"At that time," said Jesus, everybody "will see the Son of Man coming in a cloud with power and great glory."

Believers in Jesus should watch very carefully for these

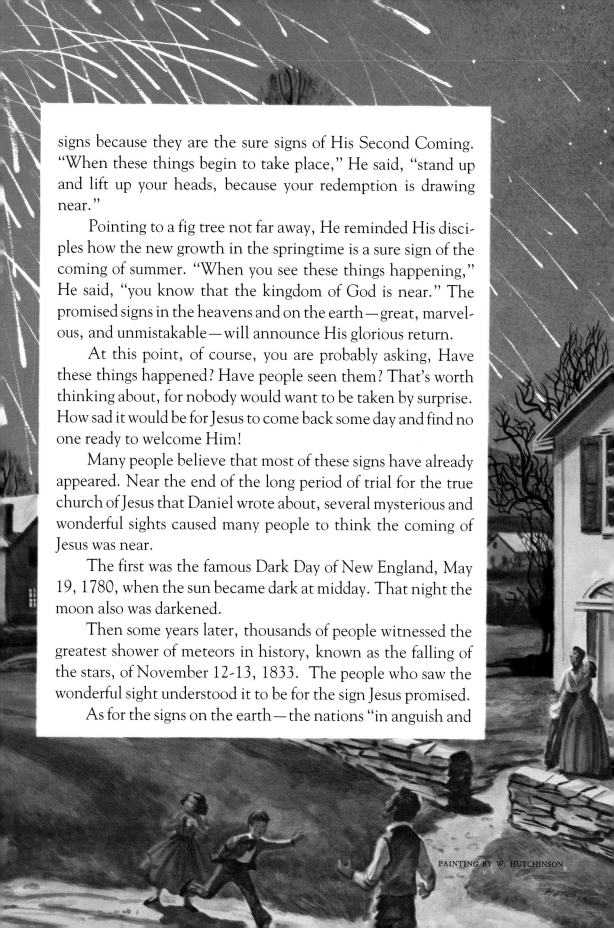

signs because they are the sure signs of His Second Coming. "When these things begin to take place," He said, "stand up and lift up your heads, because your redemption is drawing near."

Pointing to a fig tree not far away, He reminded His disciples how the new growth in the springtime is a sure sign of the coming of summer. "When you see these things happening," He said, "you know that the kingdom of God is near." The promised signs in the heavens and on the earth—great, marvelous, and unmistakable—will announce His glorious return.

At this point, of course, you are probably asking, Have these things happened? Have people seen them? That's worth thinking about, for nobody would want to be taken by surprise. How sad it would be for Jesus to come back some day and find no one ready to welcome Him!

Many people believe that most of these signs have already appeared. Near the end of the long period of trial for the true church of Jesus that Daniel wrote about, several mysterious and wonderful sights caused many people to think the coming of Jesus was near.

The first was the famous Dark Day of New England, May 19, 1780, when the sun became dark at midday. That night the moon also was darkened.

Then some years later, thousands of people witnessed the greatest shower of meteors in history, known as the falling of the stars, of November 12-13, 1833. The people who saw the wonderful sight understood it to be for the sign Jesus promised.

As for the signs on the earth—the nations "in anguish and

PAINTING BY W. HUTCHINSON

perplexity," men fainting "from terror" as they look at "what is coming on the world"—can they not all be seen now?

Grandpa and Grandma can tell you about the dreadful world wars they remember. Other wars have been fought since then, and everyone is afraid of the nuclear and chemical weapons and all the other frightening weapons with which nations threaten each other. Yes, and the jets roaring overhead tell us that the worst things we've ever feared could happen so quickly we'd scarcely have time to think what to do.

Perhaps it was because Jesus, the Prince of prophets, could see what was going to happen in the long years ahead that He urged His disciples to make sure they did not become too careless or too busy to watch for the signs of His Coming. He didn't want them to fail to see the signs, big and plain though they might be. He didn't want that day of days to spring suddenly on them like a trap that captures an unwary animal.

"Be always on the watch," He said to them and to us, "and pray that you may be able to escape all that is about to happen, and that you may be able to stand before the Son of Man."

---
* Daniel 7:25.

More Signs for All to See

(Luke 17:26-30)

AS JESUS warned His disciples to watch for His return I can imagine they said to Him, "Don't worry, Lord; we won't forget; we'll be looking for You; we'll be glad to see You again."

But Jesus knew better. He knew that after many years had passed, even those who claimed to love Him most would begin to wonder whether He would ever come back. Some would say, "My master is staying away a long time" and give up hoping for His return altogether.

Once He said that His return will be very much like the coming of the great Flood in the days of Noah. "Just as it was in the days of Noah," He said, "so also will it be in the days of the Son of Man. People were eating, drinking, marrying and being given in marriage *up to the day* Noah entered the ark. Then the flood came and destroyed them all. . . . It will be just like this on the day the Son of Man is revealed."

Everyday things will go on in much the same way as they always have right on down to the end. Boys and girls will get out

165

of bed, throw on their clothes, eat their breakfast, and run to school just as they have done all the time. Mothers and fathers will buy groceries and fix meals and go to work and clean the house. In other words, most people will be acting just about as usual "up to the day" that Jesus appears in His glory. That's why we must be so very careful to be ready for His coming all the time.

Just because life seems to go along much the same from day to day, we must never let ourselves say, "Oh, well, nothing's going to happen; the world will go on and on as it is forever." If we do, we will be taken by surprise. For Jesus will break in on us suddenly, when we least expect Him, as a thief breaks into a house at night, or as the fire fell on Sodom and Gomorrah, or as the Flood burst upon the world of Noah.

Maybe we should look a little more closely at those words of Jesus: "Just as it was in the days of Noah, so also will it be in the days of the Son of Man."

How were things back then? What were the days of Noah like?

If you want to know, just turn back to the first few chapters of the book of Genesis. Did you ever notice that after Cain killed Abel and fled eastward from Eden to the land of Nod, he built the first city? It may have been a small one, but it marked the beginning of a trend away from country living to city living with all its evils.

Did you ever notice that Cain's great-great-great-grandson Lamech was the first man to take many wives? That's when polygamy began, with all its sad results.

One of Lamech's sons, Jubal, was a great musician—"the father of all who play the harp and flute." [1] What sort of tunes he taught the people to play we are not told, but no doubt he filled the days of Noah with music of one kind or another.

His brother Tubal-Cain was skilled in the production of "bronze and iron." [2] He started the iron industry. We should not think that these men of long ago were ignorant cave men. They were closely related to Adam, who was still alive. They had keen minds and skilled hands. They must have invented all sorts of useful things, such as tools for their trades and furniture for their homes.

But despite all their skill, these men could not keep themselves from evil. Lamech boasted of killing a man who struck him. This murder led to others until the earth was "full of violence." [3]

Things got so bad that "the Lord saw how great man's wickedness on the earth had become, and that every inclination of the thoughts of his heart was only evil all the time. The Lord was grieved that he had made man on the earth, and his heart was filled with pain. So the Lord said, 'I will wipe

mankind, whom I have created, from the face of the earth.' " [4]

No doubt Jesus had all this in His mind when He said, "Just as it was in the days of Noah, so also will it be in the days of the Son of Man."

We have the city builders today, don't we? They have built many cities all around the world, each one a breeding ground of sin!

We have the makers of music, too, and what horrible music much of it is! Jubal would be ashamed of it.

We have also the mighty men of industry, with their vast iron and steel works and their factories for producing metals and machinery and weapons of every kind.

What about the family troubles of the days of Noah? Do we have those too?

Do we! Lamech married two wives, which was bad enough; but nowadays some men marry four or five times, one after another. People divorce and remarry over and over again. Families are carelessly broken up and children left motherless and fatherless. Surely Noah saw nothing quite so bad as this in the days before the Flood.

As for violence that filled the earth in those days long ago, there is more now. And it is taught in the home. Think of all the killing that goes on in the stories presented on television. All day long somebody is being shot or stabbed or poisoned.

I hope you don't look at programs that show how horrible and wicked people can be. Why? Because little by little such

pictured sin will make you think that evil isn't really evil; that there's nothing wrong about being cruel, deceitful, or dishonorable if you can get away with it. Such ideas, if you become familiar with them, will lead you away from what is right and true and beautiful. They will cause you to hate God and His commandments. Evil will become attractive, and you will begin to imagine that you can do anything you please without worrying about the consequences.

Lots of boys and girls have reached that place now. Pretty soon, as Jesus has warned us, we shall see conditions as they were in the days of Noah when "every inclination of the thoughts" of people's hearts "was only evil all the time."

So if you want to see more signs of the coming of Jesus, all you have to do is to look around you. They are everywhere. Some of them are right in your own home.

---

[1] Genesis 4:21.
[2] Genesis 4:22.
[3] Genesis 6:11.
[4] Genesis 6:5-7.

How Jesus Will Return

(Matthew 24:27-44)

TO MAKE sure that His disciples would not be misled by some false teacher, Jesus told them exactly how He would return.

He will not come secretly, He said, but openly so that the whole world may see Him. He will be as visible as lightning. "As lightning that comes from the east is visible even in the west, so will be the coming of the Son of Man."

Fog can hide a searchlight or the landing lights on an airfield, but nothing can hide lightning. The darkest clouds only help to make it seem more brilliant. Nothing will be able to hide Christ's coming, either. It will be glorious beyond words and seen by everyone.

"All the nations of the earth," Jesus said, "will see the Son of Man coming on the clouds of the sky, with power and great glory." That means everybody in Europe, Asia, Africa, the Americas, and Australia. It takes in the brown people, white people, black people, yellow people, and red people. It includes Malaysians, Americans, Arabs, Russians, Brazilians, New

Zealanders, Chinese, Germans, Indians, Africans, and everybody else. All the tribes, all the nations, all the people, without exception, will see Him come.

And He will not come silently. There will be lots of noise, so that even the deaf will know He is on His royal way. For "he will send his angels with a loud trumpet call, and they will gather his elect from the four winds, from one end of the heavens to the other."

It must have been these words of the Master that the apostle Paul had in mind when he said that the Lord will "come down from heaven, with a loud command, with the voice of the archangel and with the trumpet call of God." [1]

John remembered them too when he wrote, "The sky receded like a scroll, rolling up, and every mountain and island was removed from its place. Then the kings of the earth, the princes, the generals, the rich, the mighty, and every slave and every free man hid in caves and among the rocks of the mountains. They called to the mountains and the rocks, 'Fall on us and hide us from the face of him who sits on the throne and from the wrath of the Lamb! For the great day of their wrath has come, and who can stand?' "

Jesus, the Prince of prophets, left no doubt as to how He will return. When He comes in clouds of glory, everybody will see Him and everybody will hear Him. And there won't be any doubt as to who is coming. Everyone will know it is Jesus of Nazareth, the Messiah of Israel, the Son of God, now crowned King of kings and Lord of lords.

There's one important thing we do not know about His Second Advent, and that is exactly when He will come. The fulfillment of the promised signs tells us He is near, but the actual day is a secret known only to God. Jesus made this very, very plain. "No one knows about that day or hour, not even the angels in heaven, nor the Son, but only the Father."

After all, it's better that way. If we knew the very day of His coming, we might put off getting ready to meet Him until the night before. Many people would do just that. And they would postpone repentance until it was too late.

Not knowing the day, we must be ready all the time. And that's exactly what Jesus asks of us. "Therefore keep watch," He says, "because you do not know on what day your Lord will come. . . . So you also must be ready, because the Son of Man will come at an hour when you do not expect him."

He's going to surprise us all. I hope it will be a happy surprise for you and me. 🖊

---

[1] 1 Thessalonians 4:16.
[2] Revelation 6:14-17.

Jesus has promised that when He comes the second time everybody will see Him. Although the signs of His coming are on every hand, no one knows the day or hour of His appearing.

Radio and Television Foreseen

(Matthew 24:14)

A S JESUS talked with His disciples about His return, He gave them one other sign that could be the most important of all. "This gospel of the kingdom," He said, "will be preached in the whole world as a testimony to all nations, and then the end will come."

"This gospel of the kingdom" is, of course, the good news about His plans for the future of this world and the people who live on it. It includes the story of His coming from heaven to live among men, the story of His suffering and death, the story of His resurrection and ascension, and the story of His coming again in glory to set up His kingdom of love and restore all that was lost in Eden.

When this beautiful gospel has been preached in all the world, and everybody in all the nations has had a chance to hear it, "then the end will come."

Jesus did not say that all the people who hear the gospel will become Christians. No. What He said was that this gospel would be preached "as a testimony to all

174

nations." People everywhere would hear it and make up their minds whether or not they wanted to belong to His kingdom of love.

When you stop to think of it, this was a very wonderful prophecy Jesus made. In those days there was just one great empire in the Western world, and that was Rome. Nobody had ever heard of the United States, or Poland, or France, or the Soviet Union. England had not yet been invaded by the Roman army. China, India, and Africa were lands of mystery to most of the people of Palestine.

Yet the Prince of prophets dared to say that the glorious news about His kingdom would be carried to the ends of the earth and to nations yet unborn. Looking down the centuries, He saw them all, with all their languages, customs, and many-colored flags. "All these," He said, "will hear My gospel—and then the end will come."

He must have known that this would mean translating His message into many hundreds of different languages—but that did not trouble Him. It would be done, and it has been done.

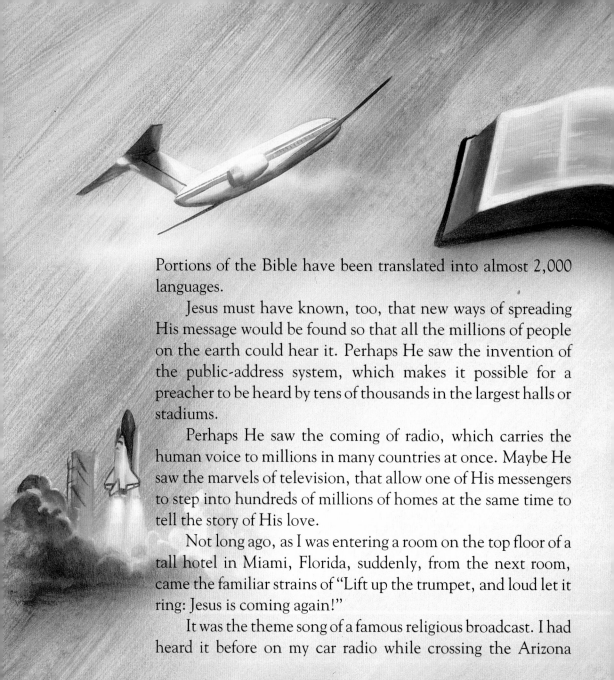

Portions of the Bible have been translated into almost 2,000 languages.

Jesus must have known, too, that new ways of spreading His message would be found so that all the millions of people on the earth could hear it. Perhaps He saw the invention of the public-address system, which makes it possible for a preacher to be heard by tens of thousands in the largest halls or stadiums.

Perhaps He saw the coming of radio, which carries the human voice to millions in many countries at once. Maybe He saw the marvels of television, that allow one of His messengers to step into hundreds of millions of homes at the same time to tell the story of His love.

Not long ago, as I was entering a room on the top floor of a tall hotel in Miami, Florida, suddenly, from the next room, came the familiar strains of "Lift up the trumpet, and loud let it ring: Jesus is coming again!"

It was the theme song of a famous religious broadcast. I had heard it before on my car radio while crossing the Arizona

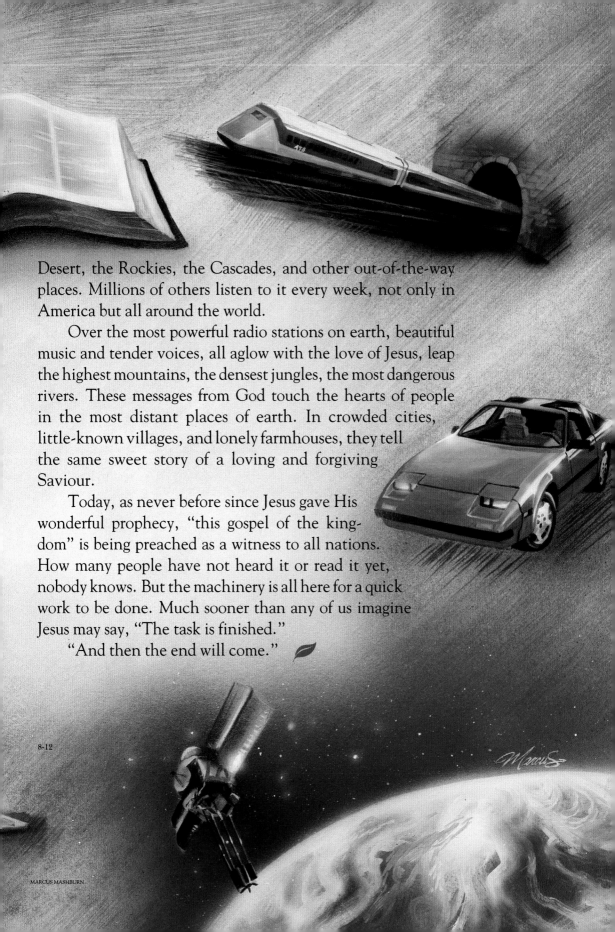

Desert, the Rockies, the Cascades, and other out-of-the-way places. Millions of others listen to it every week, not only in America but all around the world.

Over the most powerful radio stations on earth, beautiful music and tender voices, all aglow with the love of Jesus, leap the highest mountains, the densest jungles, the most dangerous rivers. These messages from God touch the hearts of people in the most distant places of earth. In crowded cities, little-known villages, and lonely farmhouses, they tell the same sweet story of a loving and forgiving Saviour.

Today, as never before since Jesus gave His wonderful prophecy, "this gospel of the kingdom" is being preached as a witness to all nations. How many people have not heard it or read it yet, nobody knows. But the machinery is all here for a quick work to be done. Much sooner than any of us imagine Jesus may say, "The task is finished."

"And then the end will come."

8-12

Ten Sleepy Girls

(Matthew 25:1-13)

ONE OF the most exciting stories Jesus told was about 10 sleepy girls. They were bridesmaids, all dressed up for a wedding, all eager to take part in it, and half of them never got there!

Since the ceremony was to be held in the evening, each girl had a little oil lamp to carry. I am sure all of them looked forward eagerly to taking part in the procession, but five of the girls took extra care to be ready for whatever might happen. They each brought along a little extra oil, just in case it might be needed.

Since it was an Eastern wedding, they were all waiting at the bride's house—not for the bride, but for the bridegroom. It was the custom for him to come to the home of the bride and lead her away to his own.

The girls weren't sleepy at first, of course. I suppose they were as happy and lighthearted as most bridesmaids usually are as they talked about the bride, the bridegroom, and their own chances of getting married.

178

Standing on tiptoe, they looked down the street for the procession to come. But as time went on and the bridegroom did not appear they began to yawn and grow drowsy. They sat down on the grass and grumbled at the delay.

"Whatever happened?" sighed one. "I wish the bridegroom would hurry up."

"I'm going to have five minutes' sleep," said another. "I'm tired; wake me up, girls, when you see him coming." She lay down and was soon fast asleep. Another girl found a comfortable spot for a nap. Then another and another until "they all became drowsy and fell asleep."

Hour after hour went by, and the 10 sleepy girls slept on.

Suddenly, at midnight, they heard somebody shouting, "Here's the bridegroom! Come out to meet him!"

The girls stirred and awoke. They rubbed their eyes. The procession was coming down the street. They jumped to their feet, straightening their dresses and patting their hair in place. Then they remembered their lamps. Quickly the girls began to trim them, for the wicks were thick with carbon.

Then five of them made a terrible discovery. They were running out of oil. "Give us some of your oil," they begged the others. "Our lamps are going out."

"Sorry," they answered, "but we don't have a drop to spare."

"But what shall we do? We'll miss the wedding!" cried the five who had no oil.

"Better go and buy some," the others said.

"What? At this time of night?"

"There might be a store open. You could try."

Frantically the five dashed off into the darkness. While they were gone the bridegroom arrived. The bridesmaids who were ready went in with him to the wedding feast. And the door was shut.

Then the saddest thing happened. The five girls who had gone to look for oil came back, breathless with running. But they were too late. They had missed both the procession and the wedding banquet.

They banged on the door, crying, "Let us in, let us in!" But nobody opened it. The bridegroom merely called from inside, "I don't know you."

The lesson here is that we must always be ready for His return. Once the Bridegroom has arrived, it is too late to find what we need to make our hearts ready for Him. And we can't expect others to make our preparations for us, either.

"Therefore keep watch," Jesus said, "because you do not know the day or the hour." It could well be that as the Prince of prophets, He was looking down the long, long years to our time. Perhaps He was thinking of you and me, knowing how easy it is for us to give up hope in His coming and become careless in our preparations for Him.

"Watch!" He says to us. "Keep awake! Look out for the signs of My return!" Someday the cry will be heard again, "The Bridegroom is coming!" From city to city, from country to country, the wonderful news will spread like wildfire, "Jesus is coming!"

Some will be ready to meet Him, some will not. Some will go to heaven with Him, and some will be left out. In which group will you be?

Let us all be ready with plenty of oil and with our lamps trimmed and burning when He comes.

Tale of the Talents

(Matthew 25:14-30)

KNOWING that He would soon be leaving His disciples and going away for a long, long time, Jesus tried to give them all the good advice He could so that they would know what to do while He was gone.

That is why He told them the story of the 10 sleepy girls. He wanted them always to be ready for His return. But just being ready was not enough. They must make the most of their lives, serving God faithfully every day and using every chance to tell others of His love.

To make this plain, Jesus told another story. This was about a merchant who went on a long trip to a country far away. Before leaving, this man called three of his servants and handed each of them a certain amount of money—"each according to his ability" to use it.

To one he gave five talents of money, to another two talents, and to the third, one talent (a talent is worth more than $1,000). Then, after urging each to do his best, he went on his journey.

The man with the five talents started to work at once, buying and selling until he had made his five talents 10. The man with the two talents did the same, only he didn't earn quite so much. Even so he made a 100-percent gain, so that his two talents became four.

But the man with one talent merely dug a hole in the ground, buried his talent, and took life easy. He told his friends that he didn't see why he should work while the boss was away on a vacation.

Eventually the merchant returned and called his servants to report on what they had done with the money he had entrusted to them. The first came and told how he had traded with the five talents and earned five more.

"Well done, good and faithful servant!" said his master. "You have been faithful with a few things; I will put you in charge of many things."

Then the second servant told what he had done. " 'Master,' he said, 'you entrusted me with two talents; see, I have gained two more.' "

"Well done, good and faithful servant!" said the master. "You have been faithful with a few things; I will put you in charge of many things."

Finally the one-talent man came to report. He was a surly sort of fellow. "Master," he said, "I knew you were the kind of man who just makes profit out of other men's work, so I buried your old talent. Here it is. Take it. You can have it back."

The merchant was very disappointed. "You wicked, lazy servant!" he said. "You should have put my money on deposit with the bankers, so that when I returned I would have received it back with interest." Then he added, "Take the talent from him and give it to the man with the ten talents. And throw this worthless servant outside in the dark."

There is a lesson here for all of us. The merchant in this story is Jesus. He has gone to a country far away. And to each of His disciples He has given talents, according to his or her ability. Some have five talents, some two, some only one. But

He expects all of us to use them the best we know how. Someday, when He returns, He is going to ask us what we have done with all the good gifts He has given us.

Oh, but you say, He never gave *me* any money.

Maybe not. But money isn't the only talent. Your voice is a talent, with the power to talk and sing. Your brain is a talent, with the power to think and plan. Your hands are a talent, with the power to write, to play music, to do good for the needy.

Stop a moment right now and count your talents. You will probably find that you have more than five, maybe 10. And Jesus wants you to use them all to His glory.

Perhaps you are saying, "But I've only got one talent." All right. Just don't bury it. Make the most of it. Use it, and watch it grow!

It's not the number of talents we have that matters, but how faithful we are in using them. Jesus wants us to be "faithful with a few things"—in even the smallest things we do for Him.

And when the day of reckoning comes, how happy you will be to hear Jesus say to you, "Well done, good and faithful servant!" That "Well done!" said with a smile and a handshake, will be reward enough for anything any of us ever did for Him.

JUSTINEN CREATIVE GROUP

Passport to Heaven

(Matthew 25:31-46)

AFTER telling His disciples to be watching always for His return and to make the most of all the talents He had given them while they were waiting, Jesus drew back the curtain of the future once more. He let them glimpse the wonderful scene when He will sit at last on His throne of glory as King of kings and Lord of lords.

"When the Son of Man comes in his glory," He said, "and all the angels with him, he will sit on his throne in heavenly glory. All the nations will be gathered before him, and he will separate the people one from another as a shepherd separates the sheep from the goats. He will put the sheep on his right and the goats on his left."

As the disciples pictured this happy day their eyes sparkled with gladness. How they wanted their Master to be a king! How they longed to see His dream of a worldwide kingdom of love come true! How they hoped that they might have a part in it some day!

But what was this about sheep and goats? Who were the

187

sheep and who were the goats? And how would Jesus separate them? Eagerly they waited for the rest of the story.

Jesus said, "Then the King will say to those on his right, 'Come, you who are blessed by my Father; take your inheritance, the kingdom prepared for you since the creation of the world. For I was hungry and you gave me something to eat, I was thirsty and you gave me something to drink, I was a stranger and you invited me in, I needed clothes and you clothed me, I was sick and you looked after me, I was in prison and you came to visit me.'

"Then the righteous will answer him, 'Lord, when did we see you hungry and feed you, or thirsty and give you something to drink? When did we see you a stranger and invite you in, or needing clothes and clothe you? When did we see you sick or in prison and go to visit you?'

"The King will reply, 'I tell you the truth, whatever you did for one of the least of these brothers of mine, you did for me.' "

These are the sheep. Christ's sheep. They stand at His right hand. They are the men and women, the boys and girls, who show kindness to others, whose hearts are filled with love and sympathy for the least important of His children. They inherit His kingdom.

And the goats? They are the little, selfish people who never give a thought to other people's needs and sufferings.

To them Jesus will say, "I was hungry and you gave me nothing to eat, I was thirsty and you gave me nothing to drink, I was a stranger and you did not invite me in, I needed clothes and you did not clothe me, I was sick and

189

in prison and you did not look after me.

"They . . . will answer, 'Lord, when did we see you hungry or thirsty or a stranger or needing clothes or sick or in prison, and did not help you?'

"He will reply, 'I tell you the truth, whatever you did not do for one of the least of these, you did not do for me.' "

For these people there will be no kingdom, no heaven, no eternal happiness. Instead they will share the punishment of the devil and his angels. Jesus said so Himself.

So it is love that makes the difference. It is love that separates those who are saved from those who are lost. It is love that decides whether we shall be among the sheep or the goats in the day of judgment.

Love is the passport to heaven. If we do not have it in our hearts—if we do not show it by gracious words and kindly deeds, we shall never enter the kingdom of God. For His

JUSTINEN CREATIVE GROUP

kingdom is a kingdom of love. It is made up of a people who love one another. And its King is the King of love.

If love is so very important, maybe we should be looking around to see whether there is anyone who needs to be loved by us. Think a moment. Is there somebody you know who is hungry, somebody whom you could feed? Maybe some poor little boy at school would be glad for a part of your lunch some day. Or a drink out of your nice new thermos bottle.

And what about the new girl in your class or the one who has just come to live next door? Are you being as friendly as you should? Have you said, "Welcome!" and meant it?

Maybe there's somebody you know who doesn't have money enough to buy clothes to keep himself warm. Could you share some of yours?

How about the sick people around you? Do you ever go to see them? Do you take them flowers or say a prayer for them?

Do you have a friend in prison? Do you ever go to see him or write him a note of sympathy?

Remember that whatever you do out of a love-filled heart, Jesus says you have done it for Him. And He will never forget the kindness. Not through all eternity.

Every time He meets you in His kingdom, He will say, "Thank you for being so kind to Me." And you will say, "Lord, when was I kind to You?" And He will smile and say, "When you shared your lunch with Tommy, when you cried with Susan, and when you visited your lonely old grandma."

And you will say, "But Jesus, I didn't think that was helping You!"

"But it was," He will say. "Whenever you loved even the smallest of My children, you were loving Me."

How glad we all will be for every deed of love we ever did!